GAME 163

WITH AN IMPROBABLE 13 WINS IN THEIR LAST 14 GAMES, the 2007 Colorado Rockies found themselves in a dead heat with the San Diego Padres for the National League's lone wild card playoff berth. Both teams had identical 89-73 records after 162 games, meaning a 163rd, played at Denver's Coors Field on October 1, would decide which squad would continue into the postseason. Not only did the teams play an extra game; they also played extra innings. The 13-inning contest lasted four hours and 40 minutes and produced 17 runs—the final one coming on a controversial play at home plate that would lead to the use of instant replay in Major League Baseball.

Like the epic battle it captures, *Game 163* has that something extra. Reliving the excitement of the game, author Denny Dressman doesn't dwell on whether or not Matt Holliday touched the plate. Rather, through interviews and scrupulous research, he stitches together a memorable quilt of events and backstories that kicked off "Rocktober" with a 9-8 Rockies win and launched a run that culminated with the team's first trip to the World Series.

"Denny Dressman long has been a respected voice and leader in Colorado's journalism and literary communities. So, his terrific *Game 163* is no surprise. The Rockies' 2007 run down the regular-season stretch to the World Series was the damndest thing I've ever witnessed in decades of covering Denver sports, and Dressman more than does it justice. His decision to make the dramatic play-in game against the Padres the pivot (not the sole focus) of his book was risky, but ultimately rewarding. Time after time, you'll go, "I didn't know that." His narrative is democratic — little "d" — with all from eventual Hall of Famers, managers, utilitymen, executives and umpires having their time in the spotlight. As he has in his previous books, both sports-oriented and otherwise, Dressman doesn't settle for a serviceable rehash. You don't have to, either. (And by the way, on the issue of whether Matt Holliday touched the plate . . .)"

TERRY FREI,
AUTHOR OF *77: DENVER, THE BRONCOS, AND A COMING OF AGE.*

"A fun, fascinating deep dive into thirteen unforgettable innings, Denny Dressman's *Game 163* delves into front-office maneuvers, clubhouse chemistry, umpiring, groundskeeping and all the other factors that decide baseball seasons—even hitting and pitching. Rockies fans will love Dressman's sketches of Tulo and the Toddfather and be tempted to add "Gags" Gallego to the Mile High pantheon. Anybody who follows the game will enjoy this smart, heartfelt, often funny book— the latest proof that there's no better story than a great ballgame."

KEVIN COOK,

AUTHOR OF *TOMMY'S HONOR*,

ELECTRIC OCTOBER,

AND *TEN INNINGS AT WRIGLEY*

Also by Denny Dressman
[NONFICTION]

Gerry Faust: Notre Dame's Man in Motion

Yes I Can! Yes You Can!
Tackle DIABETES and Win!

The Diabetes Antidote

EDDIE ROBINSON
'. . . he was the Martin Luther King of football

Sterling Heroes of World War II

HEARD but not SEEN
Richard Nixon, Frank Robinson and
The All-Star Game's most debated play

The Idea Within
David Griggs and his quest for meaning in public art

Beyond The Camps
From Japanese-American Internment Nightmare
to 'American Dream'

From The Streets of Brooklyn to Trainer to the Stars
John Parisella's Lifetime of Celebrity Connections

Charlie & Marie

Orchids & Butterflies

GAME 163

The epic '07
Wild Card tiebreaker,
and the Rockies team that
went to the World Series

Denny Dressman

COMSERV BOOKS
LLC

DENVER

Copyright © 2020
Denny Dressman

All rights reserved.
No part of this book may be reproduced in any form
or by any means without permission in writing from the author,
except for brief quotations embodied in critical articles and reviews.

For information, contact
ComServ Books
P.O. Box 3116
Greenwood Village, CO 80155-3116
www.comservbooks.com

Excerpts from the accounts and descriptions of Major League Baseball's
licensed telecast of the game between the Colorado Rockies and San Diego Padres
October 1, 2007 on TBS are used with the written consent of MLB.

The batter-by-batter account, game box score and Rockies season records
in the Appendix are published online at Baseball-Reference.com and
are reprinted with permission of Sports Reference, LLC.

Cover photo: The Denver Public Library,
Western History Collection, RMN-044-7827.

ISBN 978-0-9774283-4-2
LCCN 2020921001

Printed in the U.S.A.

*For all who ever questioned,
criticized or argued with
an umpire.*

CONTENTS

One more game 1
'Little Anthony' 11
Back to shore 21
Homegrown 33
Dealin' Dan 41
Once a phenom 55
What a debut! 67
The Dragon Slayer 75
Three runs early 85
Grand Slam 93
Expanded roster 103
'Gags' 111
Judgment call 119
Miscue 127
Three innings 133
A place in history 141
"Hells Bells" 147
"This is reality." 155
Play at the plate 165
The 'Pine Tar Ump' 175
'Holliday Touched It' 183
Three more sweeps 191

Author's Note 197
Appendix
   Game 163 Batter-by-Batter and Boxscore 205
   2007 Rockies Game-by-Game 213
   2007 Rockies Team Stats 217

*"It ain't nothin'
till I call it."*

Bill Klem

One more game

During Major League Baseball's regular season (through 2019), each team was scheduled to play 162 games over six months.

Allowing for numerous variables including the ones that end without the home team batting in the bottom of the ninth or go extra innings, those 162 games comprised approximately 1,475 innings and, on average, produced more than 8,700 outs, 1,600 runs and 3,000 hits in about 14,000 plate appearances. Between two teams, somewhere around 48,000 pitches were thrown.

It would seem that so many pitches, batters and games would separate the 30 teams in the National and American Leagues quite successfully. Indeed, experts in statistical probability calculate that it's at least a 1-in-1,311 chance that two major league teams would finish with identical records and tie for a playoff berth after a full season if they won 16 games more than they lost, i.e. an 89-73 record, as the Rockies and Padres did in 2007. At the historical tiebreaker average of 92 wins (through 2020), that chance is one in almost 12,000. So, it's a longshot . . . a rarity.

But it happens.

Some history: When the American and National Leagues added two teams (AL in 1961, NL in '62), the increase to 10 teams resulted in a schedule change from 154 games to 162. Then in 1969 Major League Baseball decided that 10 teams per league justified creating two divisions within each. By 1995 each league had expanded to 14 teams, organized into three divisions in each league. With that came a fourth playoff berth, called the Wild Card, to go to the non-division-winning team in each league with the best record.

From 1969 through 2020 (when the Coronavirus pandemic caused MLB to change its playoff structure), a tiebreaker, known as Game 163 because it's considered part of the regular season, was required on only 11 occasions to decide either a division title or the Wild Card berth in the expanded playoffs: five times in the AL and six in the NL. Nine of those 11 were Wild Card tiebreakers; two involved the Colorado Rockies (who won the first NL Wild Card spot outright in their third season).

The longest, highest-scoring and most dramatic tiebreaker in the first 25 years of the Wild Card was played October 1,

GAME 163

2007 between the Rockies and the San Diego Padres. It lasted four hours and 40 minutes and involved 44 players (21 for San Diego and 23 for Colorado). Many have called it the greatest game the Rockies ever played.

Dan O'Dowd, Rockies general manager at that time, went even further when asked, 13 years later, to describe it.

"It had historical significance in the city of Denver and the state of Colorado and the Rockies market," O'Dowd said, "but I think it had a bigger impact on the game of baseball. Looking at it now, from the 30,000-foot view, I really think it created a new era for the game of baseball, for the Wild Card, because it was such a riveting game, because it went so long and had so many emotional ups and downs, and the ballpark itself—the electricity both inside and outside the ballpark was just incredible that evening."

Pitcher Matt Herges, whose three innings of stalwart relief from the 10th through the 12th innings was one of the keys to Colorado's eventual stunning victory, expressed the feeling of virtually everyone who was part of either team.

"Who knows what the future holds, but I really don't see anything comparing to that night and how it ended, with us coming back off one of the best closers in the history of the game," he said, a reference to Hall of Famer Trevor Hoffman.

Putting the game in the context of baseball's biggest rivalry, Rockies starter Josh Fogg said: "If that's a Yankees-Red Sox game, people are talking about it as one of the greatest games ever."

After it was over, *Rocky Mountain News* columnist Dave Krieger wrote, "In all of big league history, there has never been a game like this." And when asked in 2020 how he would characterize it, sportscaster Don Orsillo, who called the play-by-play on the TBS telecast, began with one word: "Epic."

That amazing, one-in-a-thousand-plus dead heat did not occur routinely, as if one ever could after such a long season. In order for the two teams to finish with identical 89-73 records, here's what happened:

- The Padres lost their last two games when one more win would have clinched the Wild Card, including an 11-inning 4-3 defeat in Game 161 that saw the tying run score in the bottom of the ninth with two out and two strikes on the batter—who, as only baseball fate would have it, was none other than the son of the greatest Padre of all-time: Tony Gwynn Jr.

- The Rockies, who were nine games under .500 in mid-May, won 13 of their final 14 games, including an 11-game winning streak that featured a three-game sweep of the Padres IN SAN DIEGO, followed by another AT DODGER STADIUM, where the Rockies hadn't won even 40 percent of their previous games.

GAME 163

From September 16 to the end of Game 163, the Rockies had a team batting average of .319 on 163 hits—11.6 per game, including 21 home runs and 34 doubles—and averaged 7.3 runs per game. Matt Holliday hit .442 during that stretch, Garrett Atkins .400 and Todd Helton .386. Leadoff man Willy Taveras, whose batting average stood at .320 (with 33 stolen bases) on September 8, was sidelined with a groin injury throughout the streak, but his primary replacement, Ryan Spilborghs, hit .390 in his stead.

Colorado's improbable blitz to Game 163 began loudly but otherwise inconspicuously with a 13-0 rout of the Florida Marlins on Sunday, September 16. At the time the Rockies had lost three in a row, which dropped their season record to a modest 77-72, and they were fourth, 4½ games behind San Diego in the race for the Wild Card spot in the first round of the National League playoffs.

"We were backed into a corner," Clint Hurdle, then the Rockies' manager, said when recalling 2007's frantic finish. "We had to win every game. We didn't talk a lot about it. We knew it. I kept telling them, 'We haven't gotten hot yet. And we're gonna get hot.'"

A four-game sweep of Los Angeles—a first in the history of Coors Field—followed that laugher against the lowly Marlins, whose record dropped to 65-84 that day en route to a 71-91 finish. The Dodgers series began with a day-night doubleheader on Tuesday, September 18.

"Going into that," Helton said, "that's when you really start thinking, 'We have to win both these games.'"

And they did. In the afternoon, Jeff Francis increased his club record for victories by a lefthanded pitcher to 16, winning 3-1, and that night, Helton hit a two-out, two-run homer in the bottom of the ninth for a 9-8 victory.

That walkoff, as it turned out, was a harbinger of the two incredible weeks to follow. Rockies batters had not managed even one hit against Dodgers closer Takashi Saito all season, and he ran their record to 0-for-16 by quickly retiring the first two batters he faced. But then Holliday lined the first pitch he saw to right field for a single. Up stepped Helton, who had stroked the 300th home run of his thus-far 11-year career that Sunday against the Marlins—becoming the first player in club history to hit that many for the Rockies.

Saito's first pitch to the Colorado first baseman, whose batting average was .313 (his tenth straight season over. .300) but who was 0-for-4 in the game, was a called strike. The next pitch was low. Helton's swing on Saito's third pitch was typical Helton; he slashed a foul into the stands beyond third base. Ahead in the count, a ball and two strikes, Saito went hunting for strike three with a slider. Unfortunately for him, it hung.

As ballplayers like to say, Helton "barreled it." The towering drive landed well up in the seats above the out-of-town scoreboard in right, securing the Rockies' eighth last-at-bat victory of the season. As he neared the mob of jumping teammates awaiting him at home plate, Helton uncharacteristically tossed his batting helmet in the air then jumped into the teeming mass at home plate.

"It's what he's been waiting 10 years for," Atkins, the on-deck hitter, said after the game. "Then he did a stage dive. I couldn't believe it."

"When you are in a situation like that, why would you want to keep your emotions in?" the usually laconic Helton asked a reporter post-game. "I have never felt like that before."

Holliday, who set the stage by breaking through against Saito, said: "It's one of my favorite moments ever. It's something I will remember for the rest of my life."

"For the team to react from the dugout the way they did," said Hurdle, who watched from the top step, "and for Todd to react the way he did from third to home, it was goose bump time. You felt like, 'Okay. This is special. We can do this.'"

O'Dowd and Rockies president Keli McGregor felt it, too.

"That home run he hit against Saito started that whole run," O'Dowd said. "We NEVER hit Saito. Every time Saito came in the game at Coors Field, I packed up my stuff and headed back to my office because he was that automatic. So that was a special home run Todd hit. That game was like an out-of-body experience. Something was different about it.

"Keli McGregor was one of my dearest friends. He was just

a wonderful human being to work for and work with. He called me after those two wins. I had just pulled into a spot in the parking lot at the stadium, and he said, 'I've been up all night.'

"I go, 'Why?'

"He goes, 'I'm just telling you: I've got this feeling. We're about to go on a run like you've never seen before.'

"I'll never forget; his comment was: 'Buckle up.' And it happened, exactly the way he said. It happened—like he had some kind of clairvoyant vision about it. Clairvoyant, in the sense that everything he said came true."

The series in San Diego began with a 14-inning, 2-1 thriller decided by lefthanded-hitting Brad Hawpe's surprising home run off cross-firing lefty Joe Thornton, and concluded with Francis' 17th victory, which tied him at the time with Kevin Ritz and Pedro Astacio for most victories in a season by a Rockies pitcher. After three wins in San Diego it was on to Los Angeles.

Colorado had played 44 series in Dodger Stadium since the franchise's birth in 1993 and had swept the storied home team only twice. Of 110 previous games at Chavez Ravine, the Rockies had won only 42, a winning percentage of .381. But the magic continued for three more games: 9-7, 2-0 and 10-4.

The 11-game winning streak had pulled the Rockies within one game of the Wild Card with three games remaining—against the first-place Diamondbacks, who needed one win against the Rockies to clinch the NL West. As Colorado headed home after finishing off the Dodgers, the Padres were beginning a four-game series in Milwaukee. The Brewers still had a chance to catch the Cubs in the race for first place in the NL Central, which meant San Diego would be facing a team with something still to play for. These four games were the last of a seven-game, season-ending road trip for the Padres.

San Diego won the first game of that series to lead Colorado by a full game going into the final weekend. And when Arizona beat the Rockies 4-2 to clinch the NL West that Friday, September 28, while the Brewers were being eliminated by San Diego 6-3, it appeared as though Colorado's amazing finish would fall just short. The Rockies were two games behind with two to play.

"It was hard," Hurdle admitted. "They clinched on our field. They jump up and down. You feel like you'd put so much into it, and we'd gotten close. However, it's like, 'We got this far. Let's play it out. Who knows?' At least, that was my thought.

"I didn't go to that place where we're done. I did not go there. We just got beat that night. It was the first time in quite some that we came up short. I'm thinking, 'You know, until we're out, we're not out. The schedule says we're not out. They gotta lose two; we gotta win two. We'll see what happens.'"

Baseball being the unpredictable game that it is, the unimaginable happened.

'Little Anthony'

THE LIVES OF TONY GWYNN AND BUD BLACK, along with Tony's son, Tony Jr., had intersected often before Saturday, September 29, 2007. Tony Sr. and Bud were teammates in 1979 at San Diego State University (Bud a senior, Tony a sophomore) and are members of the SDSU Sports Hall of Fame. Both would make it as big-league ballplayers with long careers (Tony playing 20 seasons for the Padres and Bud pitching for five teams over 15 seasons), and they would face each other during four of those seasons. Tony Jr. was born after the 1982 season, both his dad's and Bud's first year in the major leagues. By 2007, Bud had seen his friend's son grow into a young man, as well as a big-leaguer in his own right.

"We sort of went our separate ways for a decade or so when I was in the American League and he was in the National

League," Bud, in his eighth year as Padres manager, said when interviewed upon Gwynn's early death in 2014. "But we'd run into each other over the winter at State, at football games or basketball games, and we'd catch up a little bit. He was very proud of Tony Jr."

The only player in Western Athletic Conference history to be all-conference in two sports, Tony Gwynn was drafted in both baseball (third round by the Padres) and basketball (as a point guard by the National Basketball Association's erstwhile San Diego Clippers). While becoming one of only 16 players in major league baseball history to play at least 20 seasons for the same team (when he retired after the 2001 season), he won eight batting titles (equaling Honus Wagner's National League record), led the NL in hits seven times, became one of only 32 hitters with 3,000 or more career hits, never finished with a batting average lower than .309 in a full season and had a career average of .338. Most amazing of all, Gwynn never struck out more than 40 times in a season.

He was a 15-time all-star, played in the only two World Series in the Padres' first 50 years, and (as of 2020) was one of 57 first-ballot Hall of Fame selections. He became known as Mr. Padre, a fitting sobriquet if ever there was one, and a statue of him was erected at Petco Park when it opened in 2004. After multiple surgeries, chemotherapy and radiation treatments, Gwynn died of parotid (salivary) gland cancer. He was only 54.

A public memorial service that was held in his honor at Petco Park on June 26, 2014 attracted 23,229 fans.

"It was a special relationship that both community and Tony gave to each other," Black said in tribute, "probably more so than any other athlete I can think of. Tony was special to San Diego, and San Diego treated him special back. What a tremendous guy. He WAS San Diego."

Black, whose first season as San Diego manager (succeeding Bruce Bochy) was the Game 163 year of 2007, won 121 games in his playing career—87 combined pitching for Kansas City, Cleveland and Toronto in the American League, and 34 during four seasons in the National League, where Tony Gwynn starred. From 1991 through 1994, when Bud pitched for San Francisco, he and his friend faced each other 15 times in five games. Black held Gwynn to four hits in those 15 at-bats, a .267 average—well below that career .338. Tony scored twice, each time on the front end of a two-run homer.

It wasn't Tony Sr. vs. Bud that Saturday afternoon in Milwaukee, but it was "a Gwynn" vs. "Bud's team" when Tony Jr. stepped in to face Trevor Hoffman, the future Hall of Fame closer, with the Brewers on the verge of losing and the Padres about to clinch the Wild Card. Tony Sr. was watching, torn between rooting for his son and pulling for his old team.

Hoffman already had struck out Prince Fielder and pinch-hitter Laynce Nix (whose younger brother Jayson coincidentally was in the Rockies farm system at the time). In between, Corey Hart had laced a line-drive double to left. With the tying run at second base and two down in the bottom of the ninth inning of a 3-2 game, Brewers manager Ned Yost sent the kid who'd grown up in the San Diego clubhouse to pinch hit for centerfielder Billy Hall. It was the second time Yost had played a left-on-right card in the inning.

A backup catcher in his limited playing career, Ned Yost amassed a season's worth of plate appearances over six seasons. His lifetime line reads: .212 batting average, 16 home runs and 64 runs batted in. He was considerably more successful in 16 seasons as a manager, guiding Milwaukee to its first plus-.500 seasons in 15 years in 2007-08, and later winning back-to-back American League championships and the 2015 World Series during nine years in Kansas City. He was finishing his fifth of six seasons as Brewers manager in 2007.

Yost's choice to pinch hit with the season on the line was just 10 years old when Trevor Hoffman came to the Padres in 1993—the beginning of a stay in San Diego that lasted almost as long as Junior's dad's. In 16 seasons with the Padres, spent mostly in the role of closer, Hoffman appeared in 902 games and recorded 552 saves. When Tony Jr. was growing up in his dad's workplace, Hoffman called him "Little Anthony"—reminiscent of the stage name of Jerome Anthony Gourdine, the singer with the high-pitched voice who had a string of pop hits

Game 163

(most notably "Tears on My Pillow" and "Goin' Out of My Head") with the doo-wop group The Imperials. Hoffman became one of Junior's best friends on the team. They tossed football before games and ran sprints together.

"It's kind of awkward," this "Little Anthony" told a reporter after the game. "You grow up rooting for the Padres your whole life, and now you're in a situation where you can possibly hurt their chances of getting into the playoffs."

As batter and pitcher square off, though, nostalgia has no place. Elite athletes know only to compete, to try to prevail. "As tight a ball game as it is," Hoffman said then, "your emphasis is on winning and executing pitches."

Coming to the majors with Milwaukee, not San Diego, Tony Jr.'s first major league hit had come the previous year on July 19, the exact date 24 years earlier that his famous dad had gotten his first major league hit. Both were doubles. He had since collected 44 singles, four doubles and two triples. As he stepped to the plate in the 883rd game of 1,035 in which Hoffman would pitch (for three teams) over 18 seasons, he was 51-for-199, a .256 batting average—in exactly 100 games.

Hoffman's once youthful playmate worked the count to two balls and two strikes. Hoffman could send San Diego into the playoffs with one more pitch if he either struck out his former teammate's son or induced some other kind of out. To that point, 24-year-old Tony Jr. had faced a major league pitcher 214 times. In his second big league season, he had 39 career strikeouts along with those 51 hits.

"Little Anthony" had faced Hoffman once before. It was in May of this same 2007 season, in the first game Junior had ever played in San Diego. That time he lined a fastball for a single, but the hit didn't influence the outcome, a 3-0 Padres victory over the Brewers. It did, however, reflect Junior's familiarity with the Padres' money closer. "Little Anthony" had gotten to know the way Trevor attacked hitters.

"Just watching him pitch for so long, I knew his tendencies were a little different with runners on base than with nobody on," Tony Jr. said after the September 29th game. "I knew what his tendencies were, but everybody knows what his tendencies are, and it still doesn't seem to work out for most people."

Hoffman went with a changeup, the one known as possibly the best in baseball at that time. Tony Jr. lined it deep into the right field corner and wound up on third base with a triple, his second of the season. The game was tied 3-3.

"It's quite ironic that it was Junior," was all his dad's former SDSU teammate said.

In their luxurious clubhouse, Rockies players were following the game in Milwaukee, and the 47,368 fans at Coors Field had been anxiously watching the scoreboard as they awaited the start of the game they'd come to see. For the longest time it appeared to Colorado fans that their Rockies would be eliminated before

GAME 163

they could even begin what was to be an 11-1 victory over the newly crowned NL West champs. But then came word of Tony Gwynn Jr.'s triple tying the game in Milwaukee in the bottom of the ninth. (Ironically, Trevor Hoffman would finish his illustrious career with those Brewers, recording the last 47 of his 601 saves in 2009-10.)

San Diego could still win in extra innings, but at least there was a glimmer of hope. Much of Denver held its collective breath.

Joe Thatcher, the lefty reliever who gave up Hawpe's game-winning homer in the 14th inning eight days earlier, entered the game against the Brewers in the 11th. Awaiting were the 3-4-5 hitters in Milwaukee's lineup. Ryan Braun, who would be voted NL Rookie of the Year over the Rockies' Troy Tulowitzki, led off with a line drive double to deep left. Prince Fielder then was walked intentionally, despite being a lefthanded hitter facing lefty Thatcher, to set up a possible double play. But Corey Hart hit a fly ball to deep center that enabled Braun to tag up and advance to third with one out. Bud Black had no choice but to move his infield in to cut off the winning run if possible.

Laynce Nix had remained in the game after pinch hitting, unsuccessfully, ahead of "Little Anthony" in the ninth. He was next up, but manager Yost, again playing the baseball percentages, chose another favorable matchup. He replaced the lefthanded hitting Nix (who was 0-for-10 since his September callup) with little-known Vinny Rottino, a 27-year-old righthanded-hitting utilityman who was appearing in the 17th game of what would be an unremarkable 62-game major league career. Swinging at Thatcher's first pitch, Rottino bounced a single through the drawn-in infield between third and short, and Braun trotted home. Final score: Brewers 4, Padres 3.

Black had a choice heading into Game 162: start eventual Cy Young winner Jake Peavy one day ahead of his normal turn to pitch or go with journeyman Brett Tomko. A stretch-drive acquisition, Tomko had pitched well for the Padres (2-0, 3.32 ERA) since coming from the Dodgers, where he'd been far less effective (2-11, 5.80 ERA). Black went with Tomko, figuring he'd have his ace for Game 163 if it came to that. And if it didn't, he'd have him to start the first game of the playoffs.

In Denver, meanwhile, a mid-season callup, 23-year-old Ubaldo Jimenez, started No. 162 for the Rockies. One of the replacements for three starters lost to injuries for the season (Aaron Cook, Rodrigo Lopez and Jason Hirsch), Jimenez had joined the rotation a week after the All-Star break and had split eight decisions in 14 turns. Signed as a 17-year-old in the Dominican Republic in 2001, the lanky righthander was known for his blazing fastball, which frequently was clocked at 96 miles per hour. The next season, his first as a full-time starter, Jimenez threw more pitches over 95 mph (1,342) than any other pitcher,

GAME 163

and in 2010 he was one of only three starters (along with Justin Verlander and Stephen Strasburg) to exceed 100 mph on 20 or more pitches. On April 17, 2010 he pitched the first no-hitter in Rockies history, shutting out Atlanta 4-0.

Jimenez allowed only one hit and struck out 10 Diamondbacks but left the game after back-to-walks with one out in the seventh inning set up Arizona to tie a 1-0 game. A three-run rally in the bottom of the eighth—the key hits by Garrett Atkins and Brad Hawpe—put the Rockies ahead 4-1. But Manny Corpas, who had taken over for Brian Fuentes as closer in mid-season after Fuentes blew four save opportunities in a row, was shaky in the ninth. He allowed two runs before making an exceptional play on a dribbler by lefthanded-hitting Stephen Drew to nip him at first for the final out in a 4-3 victory. Meanwhile in Milwaukee, Tomko had reverted to his Dodger form, allowing five runs in less than five innings. The Padres bullpen gave up six more as the Brewers won 11-6.

"In the clubhouse," Herges recalled, "it was a feeling of 'Ya gotta be kidding me.' But it wasn't a fearful 'Ya gotta be kidding me.' It was like, 'Holy crap! Look what we get to do now.' I don't think anyone sat there and thought, 'Oh, no. The Padres are better than us.' No. It was, 'We're gonna win that game, and we're gonna keep going.'"

Every storybook saga needs a name. In the newsroom of the *Rocky Mountain News*, a headline writer came up with

"Rocktober." It captured the improbable month that began with Game 163 and extended to the World Series.

That one-in-a-thousand-plus chance had been realized ahead of schedule, according to Bill Geivett, who had played a key role in developing the core of the Rockies as Director of Minor League Operations from 2002 to 2005.

"We really thought, looking at our player personnel, that 2008 was our year," Geivett said in an interview in 2020. "That's the year where we thought some of the younger players—Tulo, Hawpe and all those guys—would just kinda settle into the league and really compete, and we could battle with the best teams. That big run we had kinda shook all that up.

"You'd love to be able to say, as a front office, we planned it that way, but if somebody tells you it was all by design, they lied to you. Probably four years out, three years out, we had 2008 as the year when it would all come together. Those guys, with their talent, and just the group, that mentality of playing together, they certainly sped up the timetable."

Back to shore

WHEN 31-YEAR-OLD KELI MCGREGOR joined the Rockies as senior director of operations in October 1993, many people thought the expansion baseball franchise had hired a football guy. McGregor—a strapping six-feet-eight and 250 pounds—was a two-time all-conference tight end at Colorado State University and second-team All-America in his senior year. He had played two seasons in the National Football League (one with the Broncos, who chose him in the fourth round of the 1985 NFL draft), and had been an assistant football coach at the University of Florida during the 1988 and '89 seasons.

But what the Rockies really had recruited, as became evident pretty quickly, was an exceptional business executive, a fierce competitor and, most of all, an inspirational leader.

"The thing that stands out about Keli," said Geivett, who

was then assistant general manager, "is that he was our leader. A real fair guy, but a tough guy. He was so nice to people and all that, that I don't think it came across how strong a leader he was: 'Do everything in a process, and really dig in and think about what you're doing and have reasons for what you're doing.' He would question you a lot."

McGregor advanced quickly within the Rockies front office: to senior vice president in 1996, executive vice president in 1998, and president of the ball club on October 18, 2001. That last date is significant in Rockies history.

The previous winter, encouraged by an 82-80 record in 2000, management had gone for broke. Hoping to buy the pitching needed to elevate that barely .500 team to championship caliber, principal owner Jerry McMorris and General Manager O'Dowd signed lefthander Mike Hampton to the largest free-agent contract in baseball history at the time—a whopping $121 million for eight years. Then they added another lefty starter, Denny Neagle, for $51 million over five seasons. Coupled with a lineup that featured Helton, Larry Walker, Jeff Cirillo and Juan Pierre, McMorris and O'Dowd thought the 2001 Rockies were positioned to contend for the National League pennant.

Neither high-priced pitcher, however, coped well with Coors Field. Hampton started his Colorado career with a 9-2 record and 2.98 ERA into mid-June and became the first Rockies pitcher ever selected to the National League All-Star team. At that point, it was looking like a brilliant move. But in the second half of the 2001 season, Hampton succumbed to the unique physical and mental difficulties of pitching at altitude, going 5-11. He finished with 14 victories, 13 losses (a career high that he exceeded the next season, with 15), a 5.41 earned run average (his first above 3.83 in eight full seasons) and a record 31 home runs allowed. Neagle was better (9-5, 4.27) but nowhere close to his best season with Atlanta four years earlier (20-5, 2.97).

From 82-80, Colorado went the other way in 2001, finishing 73-89. Coincidentally, that's the inverse of the record it took to make Game 163 in 2007. It marked the first of six consecutive losing seasons, a run that bottomed out at 67-95 in 2005 and ended, finally, thanks to 2007's glorious final fifteen games (including Game 163).

The Rockies unloaded Hampton's millstone contract after the 2002 season, though at the cost of the fine young outfielder Pierre and taking on fat contracts others wanted to unload. Neagle, too, was jettisoned, after missing half of the third season of his contract and all of the fourth because of injuries, then getting nabbed in a Denver suburb for soliciting a prostitute. The Rockies voided his contract's final year, citing a morals clause. In the seasons that followed, the Rockies slogged along with a succession of veterans past their prime who were trying to revive their careers. The composite won-lost record for 2003-06 was 285-363, a .440 winning percentage.

Keli McGregor called getting out from under the $172 million burden created by those signings, "getting back to shore." He coined the phrase during a pivotal front-office retreat at Keystone Resort after the 2002 season.

"It's like we were in a boat, and all we were doing was taking on water in the boat," said Dan O'Dowd. "We were drowning. We were not heading in a good direction. We weren't facing reality. You can deny reality all you want, but you can't deny the *consequences* of reality all you want.

"We were living in a non-realistic world about who we were. And eventually the consequences of that have a cost. We didn't have the wherewithal to do things we did; we were just thinking we did.

"Keli challenged all of us. 'We're all going to have to stay together. We're all going to jump in the boat. If we're going to drown, we're going to drown together. But we're going to work toward creating something special.' That's why at the end of that '07 season, while I was so happy for so many people, I couldn't have been happier than for Keli, because it took his courage to do that. Everything we did started with Keli's courage."

From that uncomfortable but necessary crucible at Keystone came the philosophy that produced the Game 163 season and guided the Colorado franchise into the future. The simple principle: "Build from Within." The Rockies, McGregor insisted, would never be able to afford enough quality free agents, or swing enough major trades, to construct a championship roster that way.

"He laid out our marching orders, how we were going to move forward," recalled Clint Hurdle, then less than a year into his first major-league managing job. "We were financially leveraged; it was a house of cards. We were going to reverse our financial fortunes, and we were going to invest in character as well as talent. We were going to rebuild this thing, reboot it.

"We had made some bold moves, moves that were applauded by everybody in the organization when they were made. They just didn't work out very well for us. We acknowledged that we pushed all our chips in, and it didn't work out well.

"Now, this was the spot we were in: Did we want to try to wade through this, tread water through this, muddle through this? Maybe we come out of it; maybe it gets worse. Or do we want to cut our losses at this point, make the moves we need to make with the roster, make the moves we need to make financially, and build for the future, into something better?"

McGregor's new direction had a pointed implication for Bill Schmidt, Director of Scouting, and Geivett, who by then was in charge of the Rockies' minor league system.

"Basically, Keli's message, as I recall," said Geivett, "was, 'We're a lower mid-market club, revenue-wise. So, we're going to have to have homegrown players, and we're going to have to put the emphasis there, and live or die with our homegrown players. That was the big message: We are who we are.

"Money's like speed in professional sports," Geivett continued. "It covers up a lot of mistakes. The big-market clubs, a lot of times, would make tremendous mistakes that you would never see because they were glossed over by their overall record, because they could just outspend you. And not only on big league payroll. That's a big fallacy. They're outspending you in the Dominican; they're outspending you in the draft; they're outspending you everywhere—in how many personnel they have, the minor league teams—they're killing you.

"So, for us, it was more about process and efficiency: 'We have to be really efficient with our dollars. We have to go about it the right way. We have to have reasons for what we're doing. There's a process involved that we follow.' That was the big message. And, 'we're going to develop our own players.'

"I remember talking to Billy Schmidt and going, 'Okay, here we go. If this is the route we're going, we're going to have to scout them better than anybody, and we're going to have to pick 'em better than anybody, and we're going to have to develop them better than anybody.'"

As the field manager of the Rockies in the years that followed, Hurdle came to appreciate the importance of teamwork in the vision McGregor laid out.

"It would have been impossible for any one of us to take it

GAME 163

on by ourselves," he said. "Collectively, we shared it. We shared the hurt, we shared the angst; we shared the anger. When you have clear, clean communication, it's refreshing. It's impactful. It adds to cohesion. We had those meetings all the way through, whether it was Jerry (McMorris) or Dick and Charlie (Monfort) at the top. Keli was always leading the charge.

"We were steadfast in our commitment. We had a singular message. We were connected with our messaging. There was no shadow-talking when we were separated. We locked arms. We had some disagreements, but once we made our decision, we locked arms and we were connected publicly, physically, spiritually, emotionally. And we wanted that to get into the locker room—and into the organization, just as importantly: all the employees."

To reinforce his commitment to a homegrown team and his steadfast belief that it would lead to a championship, McGregor kept a bottle of champagne on his desk—and provided one for each member of the Rockies front office. The corks, he said, would be popped the day the Rockies won the pennant.

"I still have a couple of the empty ones," Geivett said 13 years later. "I remember Keli handing out the champagne and saying, 'Someday we're going to be opening these.' It was a really interesting way to make people understand what we were playing for and what we were doing."

O'Dowd remembers the champagne, too. Of course. But another memory stands out more.

"After we clinched (the National League pennant)," he recalled, "we brought all the full-time front-office people down, and—I get goose bumps every time I talk about this—and they stood in the area between the dugout and the clubhouse, so that as the players came off the field, everyone shared in that moment. Everyone.

"That was Keli. That changed so many people's lives, because nothing in life is greater than a wonderful memory, and that created memories for people for the rest of their lives."

Keli McGregor was a multisport athlete at Lakewood High School in suburban Denver. A running back then, he walked-on at Colorado State to play for Leon Fuller; a growth spurt turned him into a tight end. In 1992 he was voted to Colorado State's all-century team, and in 1996 he was inducted into the CSU Hall of Fame.

While coaching at Florida, post-NFL, he earned a master's degree in education with an emphasis in athletic administration. He became an associate athletic director at the University of Arkansas, working for four years under Razorback-for-life Frank Broyles. A College Football Hall of Fame head coach, Broyles had left the Razorbacks sideline—after 19 seasons, 144 victories (including two Cotton Bowl wins) and a national championship—to run the Arkansas athletics department, which he wound up doing for more than two decades. During the time Keli was learning how to run a sports operation, Broyles orchestrated the university's move from the soon-to-be-defunct Southwest Conference to the more prestigious SEC in 1992.

In a mini-biography of McGregor written for the Society of American Baseball Research (SABR), Alex Marks wrote: "During his time at Colorado State University, Keli had become friends with Mike McMorris, whose father, Jerry McMorris, had become the initial principal owner of the Colorado Rockies . . . Jerry McMorris was looking for some new and fresh ideas from outside the baseball world," quoting him as saying, 'The way that Keli came in and handled everything so smoothly, and the way he worked with others in baseball, I just knew it would be (only) a matter of time before he would be the man sitting in the big chair with the ultimate authority.' (McMorris sold his interest in the Rockies to Charlie and Dick Monfort two years before Game 163. He died of pancreatic cancer in 2012.)

McGregor's profile in the 2000 Rockies Information Guide began this way: "Compared to Keli McGregor, few baseball executives can say they have as much passion for their organization . . . McGregor directs much of that ardent enthusiasm towards two areas: people and precedents."

The full-page mini-biography identified two groups of people—Rockies fans and the club's front office personnel—and said McGregor considered them the franchise's most important assets. It noted his emphasis on customer service, on keeping Coors Field the gem that it is and maintaining a family environment, and on building memories for those two groups he valued so highly (as he did in 2007 in a uniquely Keli way).

McGregor's focus on building the Rockies from within reflected his personal philosophy—"someone who always cherished people over projects, friendships over fare, above all else, relationships over records," wrote Marks in his SABR profile. Keli's legacy is expressed at Salt River Fields at Talking Stick, the Rockies' Spring Training home in Scottsdale, Arizona—which he personally designed with colleague Daryl Hall of the Arizona Diamondbacks, who share the complex. A sign at the entrance to the Keli McGregor Reflection Trail, which borders the west side of the facility, reads:

> *"No matter what your role or title, model greatness and invite others on the journey."*

Mike Gallego, the Rockies third base coach from 2005 to 2008, has this lasting memory:

"I was walking into the ballpark one day, and Keli was about 20 paces in front of me. He didn't know I was behind him, and all of a sudden, he makes a dash toward his left. And I'm like, 'Where is he going? Is there a shortcut?'

"He picks up a piece of paper, like a gum wrapper, and he crumbles it up and puts it in his pocket. We're in the guts of the ballpark; no fans are ever in there. He took pride in his organization, to the point where he had to go 10 paces to his left because he spotted a piece of paper that he obviously was going to throw away later.

"I've never forgotten that. To this day, if I go on the field and I see a piece of paper, I pick it up and put it in my back pocket."

Keli McGregor was found dead in his Salt Lake City hotel room on April 20, 2010 while representing the Rockies on a business trip. An otherwise healthy 47-year-old who worked out regularly at Coors Field, often with members of the team, he died of a rare viral infection of the heart muscle.

At Coors Field a pinstriped circle with a baseball sign emblazoned with his initials—KSM—adorns the façade of the stands above the visitors' bullpen in deep right center, joining the retired numbers of Rockies stars Helton and Larry Walker, and the historic Jackie Robinson, whose "42" hangs in all major league parks. And the Rockies named the multi-use development adjacent to Coors Field "McGregor Square" in his honor.

Homegrown

THE 2007 ROCKIES PERSONIFIED Keli McGregor's plan. Sixteen of the 27 players on postseason active rosters were products of the Rockies' farm system, including the biggest stars: Helton, Holliday, Atkins, Hawpe, Francis, Cook, Corpas and a brash rookie shortstop named Troy Tulowitzki. (Also on the bloated Game 163 roster were draft choices Ryan Spilborghs, Cory Sullivan, Seth Smith, Ian Stewart, Joe Koshansky, Clint Barmes, Chris Iannetta and Jeff Baker, and three undrafted free-agent pitchers: Ubaldo Jimenez, Franklin Morales and Ryan Speier. All contributed, many in the playoffs, too.)

The key to their success was something bred into them as Rockies farmhands.

"I have roots in New York and Montreal," Bill Geivett said, "and certainly in Montreal, whatever you produced was what was going to be on the field. Knowing that, you made sure you were teaching a team game and a team environment, and the players are responsible to the team and responsible to each other. (By 2007) we had tremendous talent, certainly; but at the same time, that team game, team mentality, is what's going to set the less-talented teams above the more-talented teams. That's a big part of the fabric of that team.

"Any time during that season you could walk into that clubhouse, into the food room, and there's probably 10 to 12 players in there, at noon. That's how close they were as a group and as a team. They wanted to achieve something together.

"You can't do it on your own. You can't play as an individual and try to achieve something. You need people around you that can call you out when you're doing something that's not right. If somebody stepped out of line, there was probably five guys ready to jump on you, and in a good way. And they took it in a good way, as a group of players, because they knew they were playing to try to win as a group."

That closeness was apparent to Geivett from Day One in 2007.

"I can see those guys in Tucson during spring training. Whether they're out on the field, their interaction—it's like no other club that I've seen, since or before. They were all in on the joke. There wasn't a faction of players that didn't belong. They were all in. And that's the thing you don't see. They were just a close group and they loved to be around each other. It was like they couldn't wait to be around each other. You don't see that around professional sports."

Reflecting on that chemistry a decade later, Ryan Spilborghs said: "That was a group of guys that spurred each other on. We're talking the kind of banter that you have after years of playing together."

The wealth of homegrown talent earned the Rockies the "Organization of the Year" award from *Baseball America*, the highly respected magazine with the motto, "Baseball news you can't find anywhere else." In recognizing the 2007 Colorado Rockies, the editor of *Baseball America*, said: "We knew they were bringing great talent through their farm system, but we certainly didn't expect it to pay off with big league success so quickly. They won with homegrown players, have more talent on the way and have maintained stability in their front office, so they pretty much have everything we look for in an organization."

If any single homegrown player elevated the 2007 Rockies to championship level, a strong case can be made that it was the player who came to be known simply as "Tulo"—Troy Tulowitzki.

Thomas Harding, Rockies beat writer for MLB.com, wrote a retrospective on the 2007 season during the Coronavirus shutdown that interrupted spring training and delayed the start of the 2020 season until late July. In it, he related the impression

Tulowitzki made on veteran LaTroy Hawkins early in training camp that February.

"It was just pitchers and catchers, and I remember sitting with Brian Fuentes," Harding quoted Hawkins, then a 12-year veteran who had signed with the Rockies in the off season. "And I remember Troy Tulowitzki walking into the locker room. I had no clue who he was, had never heard of him."

Hawkins asked Fuentes, "Who is that dude?'" Fuentes replied, "That's Troy Tulowitzki. He might be our starting shortstop," Hawkins told Harding. "I remember looking at him saying, 'He WILL be our starting shortstop.' Not many people walk into a room and I want to know who they are. He got all my attention."

Colorado's No. 1 draft choice (seventh overall) in 2005, Tulowitzki was called up by the Rockies the following August 30—after only 126 minor-league games. He got his first major league hit the next day and played in 25 games for Colorado at the end of 2006.

"We were able to take a look at him the year before as a pre-September callup," said Clint Hurdle." So, we got to see him on the field; got a good feel for him. And he got a good feel for the big leagues . . . the third deck on the ballpark . . . teammates, the clubhouse . . . command of the game at that level . . . media—all of it. So, he came in with a very good, honest self-evaluation of what he could bring and what he needed to work on."

Hawkins astutely had called it; Tulo opened 2007 as the

Rockies' starting shortstop. But it was a rough start. After 23 games, his batting average was a meager .188, with one home run and six runs batted in. But there was never a thought that he should sit or be sent back to the minors, according to Hurdle.

"That was a no-brainer," he said. "He was going to play. He was going to learn. Some of the best players in the game had slow starts. Brooks Robinson jumps to mind. There was never a conversation, 'Hey, he can't handle it.' It was, 'He's going to figure it out.' And he did."

Tulo's statistics in his first season were, to understate them, impressive. He led all major league shortstops in five defensive statistical categories: putouts (262), total chances (834), assists (561), double plays turned (114) and fielding percentage (.987—a major league record for rookie shortstops). On top of that, on April 29 he turned the 13th unassisted triple play in major-league history, during a 9-7 victory over Atlanta.

On offense, he recovered from that slow start to finish with a .291 batting average, 24 home runs and 99 runs batted in. The 24 homers and 99 RBIs were both record-breaking for rookie shortstops, topping Ernie Banks by five (NL-HR) and Nomar Garciaparra by one (ML-RBI). Rockies fans embraced him quickly, greeting him on every trip to the plate by spontaneously calling out "TU-LO!" at the end of rhythmic recorded clapping that went: *"DUNT, DUNT, DUNT-DUNT-DUNT . . . DUNT-DUNT, DUNT-DUNT . . .*

"He brought defensive strength up the middle," Hurdle said. "He brought an impact bat in the lineup . . . We had some good players. He seemed to be that piece of a puzzle that when you put that piece in, you go, 'OK, that's a team., a good team.'"

More than the numbers, Tulowitzki brought a visceral intensity that neither Helton nor Holliday, the team's biggest stars, exhibited. And despite being only 22 years old—12 years younger than Helton—his maturity enabled him to quickly establish himself as the field leader shortstops are expected to be.

"What he brought was guts," Hurdle said. "He brought a swagger and a style of play that was aggressive. He was looking to win every day, not trying to not lose. So, the edge was real. Everyday.

"And he brought the ability to challenge teammates without a lot of time in the game. He was able to do that because they watched him play. They watched him prep. They watched his effort. They watched his energy. They watched his focus. He earned their respect in a very short time. It probably started the year before. He just continued to be a force-multiplier throughout the season."

In the view of many around baseball in 2007, Tulowitzki seemed the odds-on favorite to be named the National League's Rookie of the Year. But he finished second to Milwaukee's Ryan Braun in the closest vote ever. Braun won by two points, despite his 26 errors and .895 fielding percentage at third base compared to Tulowitzki's 11 errors and record fielding percentage almost a hundred points higher at the more demanding shortstop position.

"I don't even know who won Rookie of the Year that year," Hurdle said in 2020, "but this kid should have. If he had been chosen, nobody could have argued. It should have happened for him; it didn't. But that didn't hold him back. It probably helped him to continue to sharpen his edge and play with determination, and the confidence that was so visible."

Injuries in the years immediately following 2007 prevented the long, Hall of Fame-caliber career that seemed Tulowitzki's destiny. Between 2008 and 2014 he finished in the top 10 in voting for the NL Most Valuable Player award four times, was a four-time all-star, and won two Gold Gloves (as the top defensive player at his position) and two Silver Slugger awards (presented to the top offensive player at each position). He hit above .300 four times, with a high of .340 in 2014, and slugged 161 home runs, with a high of 32 in 2009. But he played in only 781 of a possible 1,134 games.

Traded to Toronto July 28, 2015, Tulo missed 147 of 385 games in two seasons plus two months, then sat out the 2018 season with a leg injury. He realized a dream by signing with the New York Yankees in 2019 but played only five games in pinstripes. His line as a Yankee was two hits in 11 at-bats (13 plate appearances). His final game was April 3, 2019; he announced his retirement almost three months later, on July 25.

"Tulo had the talent of an all-time great, just not the durability," commented columnist Jon Paul Morosi. "For the better part of a decade, he was baseball's best player at—pitcher aside—its most glamorous position," wrote Zach Kram for The Ringer website. "A healthy Tulo would not only have been a Hall of Famer . . . but possibly an all-time great . . ." wrote Luis Torres for SBNation.

In Game 163, 22-year-old Tulo led the Rockies with four of their 14 hits (in seven at-bats) and three runs scored. He drove in the first run of the fateful 13th inning rally and scored the second, which tied the game and set the stage for the unforgettable finish that followed.

Dealin' Dan

*"I made a lot of trades there over the years,
a lot of good ones, a lot of bad ones."*

A WUNDERKIND WHEN HE WAS HIRED by the Cleveland Indians to be their farm director at the age of 28 in 1987, Dan O'Dowd was one of baseball's hottest front office prospects by 1999. The Indians had suffered through 28 losing seasons when young, homegrown stars such as Manny Ramirez, Kenny Lofton, Albert Belle and Omar Vizquel transformed them. Between 1995 and 1999 Cleveland finished first in the AL Central five years in a row (a streak exceeded only by the Yankees' nine straight in the AL East from 1998-2006), won an average of 92 games per season (including seasons of 99 and 100) and played in two World Series (losing both, to Atlanta and the Marlins).

So, when time ran out for Bob Gebhard, the man hired to build Denver's expansion team from scratch, the Rockies hired O'Dowd to be his successor as general manager. It was September 1999; O'Dowd had just turned 40, and Colorado was playing out a desultory 70-92 season under Jim Leyland in what turned out to be his only year in Colorado. (Like Hampton and Neagle a few years later, Leyland, who had led the Marlins to the 1997 World Series title, was considered a marquee hire who would elevate the Rockies merely on the strength of his own past success. But he, too, proved to be a mistake.)

O'Dowd wasted no time beginning his remake of the Rockies. He completed five trades involving 23 players in his first 44 days, including baseball's first four-team trade in 14 years. When Spring Training began on February 17, 2000, only 10 players remained from the 1999 Opening Day roster. Two popular members of the Blake Street Bombers, Dante Bichette and Vinny Castilla, were among the missing.

Almost overnight, O'Dowd became known in Denver as Dealin' Dan, and he lived up to the moniker. By the start of the 2007 season he had made more than a hundred trades and cash player acquisitions.

The 2007 Rockies directly benefitted from a dozen of those transactions. He clicked on trades that brought three valuable starters—catcher Yorvit Torrealba, second baseman Kazuo Matsui and center fielder Willy Taveras (who missed much of the

September run with an injury and was replaced so ably by Spilborghs)—and three key relief pitchers, lefthanders Brian Fuentes and Jeremy Affeldt and righty Taylor Buchholz (who all pitched in Game 163). None of the players he dealt were missed, and most barely contributed to their new teams.

Some comparatively low-cost free agent additions (starter Josh Fogg and relievers Matt Herges and LaTroy Hawkins) paid off. And his purchase of the contract of infielder Jamey Carroll from Washington for $300,000 six days before the start of spring training in 2006 had a decisive, if improbable, impact a year later in Game 163. An early-season acquisition, Jorge Julio, proved valuable during the season, and mid-August reinforcements Mark Redman and Ramon Ortiz also contributed—Ortiz historically in Game 163 after Julio faltered.

Dealin' Dan's retrospective look at these moves provides interesting insight into the building of the team that eventually prevailed in the titanic Wild Card tiebreaker.

Josh Fogg—Starting pitcher, pitched four innings and faced one batter in the fifth, allowing five runs and eight hits; 10-9 with a 5.00 ERA in 29 starts in 2007; signed as a free agent from Pittsburgh before the 2006 season:

> "A strike-thrower (59 walks in 163.1 innings), great changeup, incredible competitor, exceptional athlete. Created something in the fabric of the clubhouse on the

other four days he didn't pitch, because he had an extremely selfless heart.

"We thought it was a great value buy for us at the time. Our level of anticipation of his impact wasn't such that we thought we were adding an impact starter; we thought we were adding more of a solid contributor—while also trying to create depth, because in Colorado you never have enough depth.

"He exceeded expectations. You can evaluate Josh's pure talent one way, but he competed in a whole different way. He was revered by his teammates."

Kaz Matsui—Leadoff hitter, second baseman; went 2-for-6 in Game 163 with two doubles, including one to start the bottom of the 13th; batted .288 in 2007 and was third on the team in runs scored with 84, including the first of the 13th's decisive three; acquired from the Mets in 2006 in a trade for Eli Marrero. Once a standout utility player for St. Louis, Marrero had batted .217 in 30 games for the Rockies and hit .182 in 25 games for New York—his last major league appearances. He was released in August that same year:

"I had interest in Kaz for a while. I knew we didn't have a chance to bring him to Colorado (when he came from Japan, where he was a star). Trying to get Asian players into Colorado is not an easy endeavor. But we looked at him when he posted.

"We had some really good reports on him. And we had watched his failures. I had spent a lot of time always looking for undervalued assets because I didn't have a tremendous amount of payroll to work with in Colorado. So, I was always trying to find guys that we felt like had underachieved because of a culture or environment they might have been in.

"It was one of those deals where we really, really liked Kaz. We liked his energy, and we liked his hit-ability. We liked the fact that he and Willy Taveras, who was healthy at the time, would bring a level of speed into the dynamics of our lineup ahead of what we thought was a really good group of young offensive players. So, we felt good about that acquisition.

"A lot of people felt like we got lucky. Honestly, we didn't feel that way. We felt Kaz was a really good player who just got in a bad situation in New York, who would flourish somewhere else. And he really flourished for us. I loved the guy. I thought the guy was an incredible competitor, another guy who had absolutely no fear to compete, and he had a really good skill set. He was a good defender at second; he was consistent turning the double play.

"I thought he had the biggest hit for us in that postseason run. He took a dagger to the throat of the Phillies (in the National League Division Series). That grand slam—that day in Philly was a really unusual day, to see that many fans absolutely just go dead quiet.

"Kaz had the ability to rise to the occasion. Him getting that inning going the way he did really set the tone for the 13th (in Game 163)."

Yorvit Torrealba—Starting catcher, rated in a fan poll the Rockies' best backstop ever; homered in the second inning of Game 163; batted .255, had a .991 fielding percentage in 2007 and started 105 games, second only to Joe Girardi's 119 in 1995; acquired before the 2006 season from Seattle in trade for pitcher Marcos Carvajal, who never pitched for the Mariners and appeared in only three major-league games, for Miami in 2007, after the trade:

"There was something about 'Torre' when I watched him play. Our analytical data on him wasn't great. It wasn't an analytical acquisition. It really wasn't even an instinctive acquisition, because our instinctive intelligence group, our scouts, were just okay on him, too. There was just something about 'Torre,' for me. I thought he framed the ball low exceptionally well; thought that was really important in that ballpark.

"But there was an energy that he created from behind the plate. I think your energy as a team comes from your catcher position. I think it starts and ends there. And there was an energy that he brought, and confidence, too. We were a good group of kids, but I questioned, at times, how mean we were. He brought that to our club. He's tough; he's a tough guy. He'd fight you in a heartbeat. I thought he became the heartbeat of our club. Tulo really added that, but Torrealba added that as much as Tulo.

"In fact, that was one of the bigger mistakes I made in my career. I got into a pissing match over money and let him walk—over $750,000. That was dumb, really dumb, because 'Torre' brought something to our club that we really lacked. He's a heart-and-soul guy. A good defender, too."

Jeremy Affeldt—Situational lefthanded reliever who retired the only batter he faced in Game 163; 4-3, 3.51 ERA in 75 games in 2007; acquired from Kansas City in a four-player trade in which O'Dowd gave up first baseman Ryan Shealy, who played in 123 games for the Royals over three seasons, and pitcher Scott Dohmann, who went 1-3 with a 7.99 ERA in 21 games for KC in 2006, then signed as a free agent with Tampa Bay:

> "A failed starter. Had interest in Jeremy for years. Tried to get him multiple times.
>
> "Very difficult guy for Dayton (Royals GM Dayton Moore) to give up in Kansas City because of the innate talent that Jeremy had. But he really had failed as a starter. We always felt he was miscast as a starter. Got him, put him in the bullpen. Flat-out flourished. Went on beyond us and had an unbelievable run in San Francisco. Power lefthanded arm with a wipeout breaking ball who was an inconsistent strike-thrower, who wasn't overexposed with that issue coming out of the bullpen.
>
> "Another incredible guy in our clubhouse. Accountable, tough, no fear at all, beloved by his teammates. Just another guy you feel really good about giving the ball to in big situations."

LaTroy Hawkins—Pitched a scoreless 7th inning in Game 163; 2-5, 3.42 in 62 games in 2007; signed as a free agent in December 2006 after one season with Baltimore; Colorado was his fifth of what would total 11 teams in a 21-year career:

"We had done a ton of background work on Hawk. We knew he was one of those guys who walked the walk, called out guys, held people accountable. And we really thought he had a ton left in the tank, from just a stuff standpoint.

"He was like the icing on the cake, the cherry on top. If he felt you were doing anything that got in the way of the best interests of the team, whether that was Todd Helton or the last guy on the roster, you would not escape his wrath, in a good-natured way."

Brian Fuentes—Tough-luck reliever who pitched the 8th inning of Game 163; 3-5, 3.08 in 64 games in 2007; Rockies' all-time saves leader with 115; acquired from Seattle with two other pitchers in a trade for two-time all-star third baseman Jeff Cirillo after the 2001 season:

"We had a really good feel on him. They (Seattle) had shown interest in Jeff Cirillo. We couldn't afford to keep Jeff, financially, even though he'd been a really good player for us. We had earmarked Brian at the beginning of the winter as a guy we wanted to acquire. We ended up getting Denny Stark with him, and Denny actually did okay for us, too. Very limited market for Jeff.

"A really interesting story: I was leaving the winter meetings in Boston, on my way out of my room, when Pat Gillick called me. He was the GM of the Mariners. He asked if he and Lou Pinella could come up, and I said I had just checked out of my room. So, I went down to their room, and we ended up making the deal as we walked out of the hotel.

"We loved the uniqueness of Brian. His fastball, we thought, would be an equalizer in our ballpark. We didn't talk about spin much back then, but his spin was incredible, from a unique angle. Good kid, great competitor. We didn't know exactly what we had, but we soon found out that what we had was pretty special."

Matt Herges—Worked the first three extra innings of Game 163; 5-1, 2.96 in 35 games after mid-season callup; signed as a free agent after the 2006 season, spent with the Florida Marlins:

"We signed Matty as a minor league free agent. He went to Colorado Springs and dominated better than anybody I've seen down there, and I saw a lot of players over the years with Cleveland down there, too. His changeup was Trevor Hoffman-like. It was a lethal weapon; it played really well in our ballpark.

> "He was durable, could pitch multiple innings. Another guy with absolutely no fear. Another guy Clint could put in the game at any time and know he was going to throw strikes. Matty was a constant strike-thrower."

Ramon Ortiz—Rescued the Rockies in the 13th inning of Game 163 with 10 pitches; a mid-August addition who did not make the postseason roster; acquired from Minnesota in a trade for minor-league infielder Matt Macri, whose only major-league service was 18 games and 36 plate appearances with the Twins the next season:

> "The upper level of our system at that point in time didn't have a high level of power arms in it. We were taking a shot, trying to create as much depth as possible. We didn't give up a lot. The pitching game in Colorado is a game of attrition, so we were just trying to layer on top of layer as many experienced guys that added something to our staff that we felt like we didn't have.
>
> "Ortiz had a dominant cutter, something that our staff didn't have. That gave Clint a different look coming out of the 'pen."

Jamey Carroll—1-for-2 in Game 163 plus the game-winning sacrifice fly; batted .300 in 2006 but only .225 in 2007; contract purchased from Washington for $300,000 in February 2006:

"When you're looking to fill out the bottom of your roster, I always looked for guys that, besides the multiple dimensional aspect of it, had exceptional bat-to-ball skills. He was an elite bat-to-ball guy (which he proved in the 13th inning of Game 163). He could bring the bat to the ball anywhere in the strike zone.

"Very, very smart, high-intellect baseball player who understood his role, and also was a guy who contributed incredibly to the fabric of our club, because the way he played the game pushed other people to play the game the same way, even if he wasn't a star on the team. He played the game the right way, all the time. He was a really, really important player on our club."

Willy Taveras—Missed the last 21 games of the regular season with an injury, but activated for the NL Championship Series and World Series, and made a spectacular diving catch that was one of the keys to beating Arizona in the NLCS; batted .320, with a league-leading 27 bunt hits, and stole 33 bases in 95 games in 2007; acquired from Houston with pitchers Jason Hirsch and Taylor Buchholz in trade for pitchers Jason Jennings, who won 58 games for the Rockies between 2001 and 2006 but only four more through 2009, including 2-9 in his only year in Houston, and Miguel Asencio, who never pitched in the majors after the trade:

Game 163

"It took a ballsy decision on Clint's part to activate him when the team was playing so well. But we don't beat the Diamondbacks without Willy playing center field. That play he made in right center that night (Game 2, a 3-2 victory in 11 innings) was . . . only Willy could have made it. As well as Cory Sullivan played, and Spilly, filling in for him, neither of those guys could ever have made that play athletically. That was a great call on Clint's part.

"Willy wasn't the most durable guy, but when he played, there was an electricity. I had struggled trying to find a center fielder for years. That's a very difficult ballpark to play center field in. You can add a guy who can run, but then you can't add a guy who can hit. So, it was difficult to find that guy. We took a shot at Willy that winter, when we traded Jason Jennings and got back Willy and Buchholz, who played a huge role in our club during that run, and Jason Hirsch, who got hurt."

Dealin' Dan was also on the periphery that January of a deal that didn't happen but made a lot of headlines: the near trade of Todd Helton to the Boston Red Sox. An old saying in baseball goes, "Sometimes the best trades are the ones you don't make." The Helton saga qualifies.

"That was based on Todd's desires," O'Dowd said in 2020. "It wasn't a call we made to them. It started with a conversation Todd had with me, but quite honestly, those kinds of conversations go way above a GM's head, because you're not the one who owns the team.

"That was an owner-to-owner discussion. A lot of the owners were involved in that deal. Trading that kind of player is an ownership decision, not really a baseball decision.

"I think Todd wondered if we were ever going to win there. I understood it completely. But I think at the end of the day, he began to reflect on everything he had in Denver. Playing for one team your entire career creates a legacy that's really hard to do in professional sports anymore.

"Todd decided he really didn't want to go, which was actually really good. I don't think any of us wanted to do that. At the same time, it wasn't something we weren't going to pursue if that's truly what he wanted to do. He'd been through a lot."

As it turned out, Helton batted .320 with 17 home runs and 91 runs batted in in 2007, and he was a key player in the Rockies' late surge that ultimately carried them all the way to the World Series—against Boston.

Once a phenom

THE COVER OF THE MARCH 20, 1978 ISSUE of *Sports Illustrated* is a famous one, at least in baseball circles. It features a vibrant photo of 20-year-old Clint Hurdle in a Kansas City Royals uniform, smiling, possibly interacting with someone off-camera, his full, black hair slightly tousled. "THIS YEAR'S PHENOM," reads the heading.

Phenom is defined as "a person of phenomenal ability or promise," and inside, the cover story quotes various Royals front office types, coaches and others: "one of the best prospects I've seen in my 17 years . . . I bubble inside when I think of his potential . . . the best hitting prospect I've ever seen in our organization . . . the best player in the minors last year . . . he has the makings of a great player . . . "

"It was overwhelming," Hurdle reflected more than four decades later. "Growing up as a kid, there were three magazines when you walked into a 7-Eleven. You saw *Newsweek, Time* and *Sports Illustrated*. There wasn't a magazine rack.

"The *SI* cover was a big deal," he continued, "and to be a minor-league player and to know they have the photo shoot and to know they did a couple dozen players—that's a big deal. You don't know who it's going to be. You go through this hour-plus photo shoot. You never know how it's going to break.

"Nobody gave me a heads-up. I go to a convenience store one morning to pick up a carton of milk and a Honey Bun— my breakfast that I grab every day—and I put everything on the counter. The guy looks at me and looks at the magazine. I look at him. We stare at each other. We both try to talk, and nobody can say anything. I just walked out of the store."

Amid such glowing acclaim, the piece also recalled a similarly hot prospect from three decades earlier named Clint Hartung, a "can't miss" 6-foot-5 pitcher-outfielder in the spring camp of the 1947 New York Giants. This proved to be almost prophetic, and not only because both were named Clint.

"Rather than stop at the Polo Grounds, they should have taken him straight to Cooperstown," one writer said sarcastically after Hartung fizzled. Despite hitting .309 and winning nine games as a rookie, he was out of baseball after six seasons. He finished with a 29-29 won-lost record, a 5.02 ERA, a .238 batting average, and 14 home runs and 43 runs batted in. Baseball savant Bill James, originator of the advanced statistical analysis that dominates 21st century baseball called Sabermetrics, later created the erstwhile Clint Hartung Award (discontinued in 2000) to recognize "the most over-hyped rookie of each decade."

Clint Hurdle didn't receive the Clint Hartung Award for the decade of the '70s—James crowned pitcher David Clyde (18-33 in five seasons after going straight to the Texas Rangers as an 18-year-old). But he could have. The "Phenom of 1978" played in the big leagues for 10 seasons (if you count 1977, when he played in nine games for the Royals; 1982, when he got in 19 for the Reds; 1983, 13 games with the Mets; and 1987, three, again with the Mets). His career line reads 515 games, 32 home runs, 193 runs batted in, and a lifetime batting average of .259.

"I gave it everything I have," Hurdle said, looking back. "I wanted to make everyone happy at the beginning. In the big leagues, I lost some direction . . . tried to please too many people . . . got outside myself. Sometimes you read those articles, and you have a tendency to believe them. Then you realize: When you do well, they write well; when you don't do well, they write bad. It makes you sad, hurts your feelings, makes you mad.

"There were lessons learned. I met a lot of great people. It was a great life experience. It prepared me for what was next, even though I didn't know what was next."

The road to dugout success began at St. Lucie in the Class A-Advanced Florida State League in 1988. His team finished 74-65 that year, and improved to 79-55 the next. Hurdle credits former major-league player and manager Davey Johnson with starting him in that direction five years earlier.

"I joined Davey Johnson at Tidewater in 1983," he said. "The opportunity came up to learn how to play third base. The next year, he asked me to be a catcher. He groomed me to be a super utility player. I could play both corner outfield positions, third and first base, and catcher.

"The view from catcher was the first time I saw the field in front of me and everybody playing. It gave me a different perspective. It gave me a better lens to the game. It was during that time, playing in the major leagues my last three years, that I thought about potentially coaching or managing. I was learning from coaches, learning from managers."

As a manager, he was considerably more successful, taking the Rockies to their only World Series (through 2020) and leading the Pittsburgh Pirates to their first winning season in 21 years (94-68 in 2013). He guided the Pirates to three consecutive berths in the National League playoffs in 2013-15 and received *The Sporting News* National League Manager of the Year Award in 2013. (He retired following the 2019 season.)

"I learned as I went," Hurdle said. "I honored the name on the front of the jersey, and I honored the name on the back. I just kind of rededicated something my mother told me. I think I was five the first time she told me. I was going out to play a game, and she said, 'Give it everything you've got.' In managing, I tried to give it everything I've got."

Such a contrast between Hurdle the Player and Hurdle the Manager was understandable, at least to Bill Geivett.

"It's pretty typical in the history of the game," Geivett said. "Sparky Anderson wasn't a great major-league player. Tommy (Lasorda) wasn't a great player. LaRussa was not a great player. There's plenty of them.

"When you get treated like the best player on the team, you don't know how the other guys get treated. You don't know what it's like to get released; you don't know what it's like to be traded. You don't know what it's like to know that your future with this club may be hinging on this one at-bat. The stars can hit in whatever group they want to hit in; they can do whatever. It's the guys who are normal players that get to see everything around them.

"That's why they're the better managers.

"To me, Clint Hurdle's the best. He was the right man, at the right time. He allows the players to be the players. He knew how to let them go, and to do their thing. He's a tremendous guy at that level. He really has a great understanding of how to work with a team and with individual players. He's just got a great feel for handling major league players."

After six years managing in the Mets' minor league system (ending with two seasons at Tidewater/Norfolk in the Class AAA International League), Hurdle joined the year-old Colorado Rockies as minor league hitting instructor in 1994.

"I was embraced in that organization in 1993, in the winter, in October. Dick Balderson (Director of Player Personnel) hired me. I knew one person in the organization. That was Dick. I knew the names of probably a couple dozen people. But I only knew one person. To go from 1993, October, to 2007, it was a dream come true."

Three years after joining the Rockies Hurdle was promoted to hitting coach under manager Don Baylor. He remained with the big-league team in that capacity through the last two years of Baylor's six-year run, Jim Leyland's one season and Buddy Bell's two-plus. During that time, the Rockies compiled the two highest team batting averages in the National League in 70 years (.294 in 2000 and .292 in 2001), recorded the most hits in a season since 1930 (1,664 in 2000), set the league record for total bases with 2,748 in 2001, and set the National League record for home runs by a team with 239 in 1997.

Aside from individually designed work, Hurdle's philosophy consisted of two main points: "When you go to the plate, don't take your glove. And when you play defense, don't take your bat." (In other words, keep hitting and fielding separate.) And, "Believe that hard work does make a difference." ("My dad said this to me a long time ago: 'There's always going to be people smarter than you. There'll be people with more experience than you, and there may be people who have better players. But you should never be out-prepared, and you should never be out-worked.'")

Hurdle was named manager when Bell was fired 22 games into the 2002 season. That turn was about as unexpected as anything could be, as Clint tells it.

"Dan is the one who put his chips in, in a tough spot, to ask me to be the next manager after he made the change from Buddy.

"I actually thought he was coming over to my house that morning to fire me. He called and said, 'Can I speak with you?' We had played horribly: dropping balls in the outfield; we didn't hit; a lot of things I was in charge of or a part of. Dan said, 'I want to talk with you.' I said, 'I'll come to the park early.' He said, 'No, I want to come over to your house.' I thought, 'Holy cow! He's going to come over and fire me.'

"I'm thinking, 'That's pretty professional.' Because one of the hardest things to do in pro sports is to let somebody go in the clubhouse. They have to pack a bag and walk out. That's impactful. It's hard, because there's some embarrassment and shame to it.

"I thought, 'He's coming over to the house so that I won't have to pack that bag and walk through that clubhouse.' Then he offered me the managerial job, after he walked through his mindset and what had gone on and where he was. When a man commits to you like that, how can you not be thankful, grateful, and know you're going to give him everything you've got every day to help navigate and push through?"

To O'Dowd, the choice seemed obvious.

"I didn't want to go outside the organization once we made a change with Buddy," he said. "The ballpark itself is such a unique venue that trying to go out and bring somebody in who had no experience at all, and no understanding of the nuances, wasn't something I wanted to get in the middle of.

"I didn't know Clint at all before I got to Denver, but the more I got to know him in '00 and '01, I just believed he was a manager-in-waiting. He had great communication skills. He was very authentic as a human being. He had a unique quality of being vulnerable as a leader. You could go down and have a conversation with Clint about thought process—why—and he would never be defensive. I found that to be so rare. And I found him to be a very resilient person, and I felt like that was one of the key qualities for being a success there, because you're going to have some losses that are just gut-wrenching because of the ballpark.

"I just felt Clint was ready; it was his time. No other reason than I felt it was Clint's time."

Hurdle won his debut, 4-1 over the Phillies, on April 26, and his Rockies swept both Philadelphia and Pittsburgh to start his managerial career 6-0. But that magic didn't continue; the team finished the season 67-73 under its new leader. It was the end of the Mike Hampton mistake and, for all intents, the Denny Neagle debacle, too, and the beginning of that long slog that preceded 2007. As if he were the ultimate company man, Hurdle smiled his way through seasons of 74-88, 68-94, 67-95 and 76-86—with lineups that included the likes of Jeromy Burnitz, Shawn Estes, Charles Johnson, Preston Wilson, Ronnie Belliard, Chris Stynes, Jay Payton, Royce Clayton and many others who were trying to recapture past glory.

The manager was in no way, shape or form ever in jeopardy, O'Dowd said. "He was part of the process. When we made the ill-fated Hampton and Neagle decisions, that was painful—but also cathartic, at the same time. For the first time, the Rockies had to face the fact of who they are and where they are. We set on a long-term course of who we wanted to become.

"Losing stinks," O'Dowd continued. "There's nothing enjoyable about losing. But when you're losing toward a greater purpose, it makes it a lot more bearable than when you just losing pointlessly. We knew we were taking some significant steps *back* to make some significant steps *forward*. As bad as the '06 numbers looked, even at the end of '05 I started to see some signs that we had a talented group of guys who were ready to come up to the big-league level and settle in, and how good they were going to be.

"Only time would tell, of course. Predicting baseball is like predicting the weather. But we felt good about the core we had started to develop."

Hurdle was all in.

"They gave me the opportunity to be the manager of a major-league ball club," he said, "to be the leader of that team in the clubhouse, to represent that region of fans, to represent that organization. I was humbled to have the opportunity, and I have never been one to back away from hard work, to roll up my sleeves.

"They needed a new vision. They wanted somebody who would be part of the heavy lifting, and somebody who was positive, optimistic—sometimes to a fault. I was going to pump that in the clubhouse every day; I was going to lead by example. My goal was for my actions to be more impactful than my words, because I needed to show up every day and show a positive vision, clarity of focus and connection.

"I knew what I signed on for, because everything was laid out beforehand. There was no gray area."

In an odd way, the start of Hurdle's big-league playing career matched what happened in the last month of 2007. A September call-up in 1977, Hurdle helped as the Royals won 24 of 25 games between August 31 and September 25 to run away with the American League Western Division title. In nine games and 26 at-bats, Hurdle batted .308 with two homers and seven runs

Game 163

batted in. "It was kind of crazy," he remembered. "You get called up to the big leagues and the team never loses!"

Thirty years later it was a different experience.

"It was, for me, the most incredible ride I've ever been a part of, ever associated with," he said. "The surreal thing for me was that I wasn't playing. It was like being the dad watching your kids out in the backyard every night, and coming in and saying, 'Wow. They did it again. They found another way to win.' Every night, it was all the baseball clichés you talk about.

"There may not be too many people in the game who were part of two streaks like that."

What a debut!

Throughout the Rockies' sprint to the finish in September 2007, fans who followed game after game of the streak on television listened to Drew Goodman and George Frazier. But Game 163, while considered part of the regular season, was the first game of Major League Baseball's new postseason coverage deal with cable giant TBS. Calling Game 163 were Red Sox play-by-play man Don Orsillo and two TBS regulars, ex-major leaguer Don Simpson and the late Craig Sager.

It was Orsillo's first game on TBS, and the first nationally televised game of his career. What a debut it proved to be!

"It's the seventh one-game playoff EVER; doesn't get any better than this," he said at the start of the telecast.

Recalling that day in 2020, he said: "High-stakes battle that had everything. It was a heavyweight fight with the winner ending up in the World Series."

Posted to YouTube and available online from Major League Baseball, the national telecast of that game has been viewed tens of thousands of times since. Orsillo is among those many viewers. "MLB Network has played it quite a few times over the years," he said when interviewed, "and it always brings back the feelings I had doing that game. Nerves, mainly."

It's a bit surprising to hear Orsillo say he was nervous. The "Voice of Game 163" called more historic games than most sportscasters during 20 years as the voice of Boston baseball, on radio from 1996-2000 then on television through 2015. Among them were no-hitters by Hideo Nomo, Derek Lowe and Jon Lester, as well as iron man Cal Ripken's final game. And he was there for Boston's 2004 World Series sweep of the St. Louis Cardinals that ended the supposed curse that had denied the Sox a championship for nearly a century after cash-strapped owner Harry Frazee sold Babe Ruth to the hated Yankees on December 26, 1919.

Orsillo would succeed sportscasting legend Dick Enberg as the television play-by-play voice of the Padres—yes, the Padres—after Enberg retired at the end of the 2016 season. "In 2015 the Red Sox decided not to renew my contract, so I was a free agent for the first time in my MLB career," he said. "The Padres were very welcoming and aggressive in their pursuit, and

I was extremely pleased with the offer, ownership, and the city of San Diego, which would become my new home."

But prior to moving almost 3,000 miles from one coast to the other, Orsillo became one of four play-by-play announcers engaged by TBS for its coverage of the baseball playoffs between 2007 and 2013.

"In late August of 2007 executives from Turner (Broadcasting) came to meet me in New York, where I had an off day with the Red Sox," Orsillo recalled. They offered him a postseason series that day, but it was too early to specify which one it would be. Boston was in first place in the American League East, seven and a half games ahead of the second-place Yankees, and thus seemed a likely playoff participant (though its lead would shrink to a game and a half as late as September 23).

Orsillo didn't find out he was calling Game 163 until the night before.

"I was in Boston, finishing my last regular-season Red Sox game (a 3-2 loss to Minnesota), and TBS told me after the game to go to the airport and wait for a call. Two hours passed and I got the call to check in and fly. I asked where I was going? They said 'Denver.' Never thought to ask who I was working with.

"My first call—while I was boarding the plane from Boston to Denver—was to my Boston stats guy, Justin White. I said, 'I need bullet points on the Rockies and Padres and a season overview. Oh, and I need it yesterday. ASAP.'

"Later that night, after arriving in Denver, I got a note under my door with pickup times and game info stats. In the packet, Joe Simpson's name was also there. That's when I realized I was working with Joe."

Analyst Simpson played for the Dodgers, Mariners and Royals during a nine-year major league career. In 605 games he batted .242 with nine home runs and 124 runs batted in. His ignominious claim to fame is being Gaylord Perry's milestone 3,000th strikeout victim while playing for Los Angeles in 1978. Simpson began his sportscasting career as an analyst on Seattle telecasts in 1987, and moved to Atlanta in 1992, calling Braves games on TV or radio for more than 25 years.

"I started thinking about it while I was still playing," Simpson said of his decades-long announcing career. "Listening to the Game of the Week, I got tired of hearing the analyst always trying to tell the audience what a player was thinking. That was absurd. Made me think perhaps I could do a better job. I've been very fortunate to be a part of the game in this capacity for so long. It's the next best thing to playing, for me."

Simpson was in Houston, where the Braves were wrapping up their 2007 season (a 3-0 loss to the Astros to finish 84-78), when TBS informed him that he'd be going to Denver for Game 163 between the Rockies and Padres. He and Orsillo had never worked together before, but no one listening to them would have guessed that. "He and I really had a good cadence from the git-go," said Simpson, whose National League background was an asset.

"Joe was enormously helpful from a personal and professional standpoint," Orsillo said. "We had met a few times before, as our business is a small fraternity, but became great friends after the experience. I, as the Red Sox voice from the AL, knew very little about the Rockies or the Padres and the NL in general. He quickly got me up to speed and helped me greatly."

Atlanta had played Colorado and San Diego six times each during 2007. Simpson was in the booth for all 12 games.

"I knew both teams pretty well," he said, "and I also relied on my friend George Frazier, who covered the Rockies all year long. And Bud Black was a teammate of mine in Seattle and KC. Plus, every year I talked to a lot of scouts, prior to my assignment. Don told me to fire away whenever I had something, since I was an NL guy. That allowed me to be aggressive to the mic, when I had something to offer him."

Their exchanges belied their first-time pairing. For example:

"How about this game, Don," Simpson said familiarly in the bottom of the first. *"You've got the Pitcher of the Month for September on the mound; the Player of the Month on deck, and the guy who is the odds-on favorite for Rookie of the Year coming to the plate."*

"I think we are similar people," Orsillo said, "and I really liked him. He was welcoming, helpful, and a real team player. We realized we were in this together and got along famously. TBS, in fact, decided to keep us together for the next series after that game, for the Phillies-Rockies NLDS."

The third member of the TBS team—colorful, quirky Craig Sager—was best known for his flamboyant wardrobe and "engaging" style courtside at National Basketball Association games. He wore outlandish, multicolor jackets—more than 150—with coordinated slacks, ties and footwear (either colorful basketball shoes—more than a hundred pair, all different—or, when working baseball, Western boots, as he wore at Coors Field).

"My clothes reflect who I am," he wrote in his autobiography, published shortly before he died of a form of leukemia on December 15, 2016. "I believe that life should be fun, and so should your clothes."

For all his showmanship, though, Craig Sager was a respected, award-winning sportscaster. "Always prepared and always spot-on," Simpson said. "Craig and I were good friends, even though we didn't work together much."

A high-school classmate of former Denver Nuggets star Dan Issel, Sager was inducted into the Sports Broadcasting Hall of Fame, received the Curt Gowdy Media Award from the Naismith Memorial Basketball Hall of Fame, and won an Emmy (television's Oscar). And while he was best known for his work before, during and immediately after pro basketball games, Sager was no stranger to big baseball moments.

His first came in 1974 when Hank Aaron homered in the Braves home opener to break Babe Ruth's career home run record. "Craig was the guy in the trench coat trying to talk to Hank as he made his way to home plate!" Simpson recalled.

Working his first job after graduating from Northwestern, Sager was news director at WXLT in Sarasota, Florida in 1974, which sounds like a bigger deal than it actually was. The job paid only $95 a week, but the press pass that came with it enabled Sager to attend almost any sporting event he wanted. He was in Atlanta on his own, hoping to see history made. As Aaron rounded the bases after slugging No. 715, Sager leapt from the stands to record the moment—interviewing the new Home Run King among his celebrating teammates.

Known for coming up with unusual sidelights to every event he covered, Sager did not disappoint during the telecast of Game 163. At one point he told TBS viewers that Major League Baseball had conducted 28 coin-tosses on September 7 to decide who would have home field advantage in various playoff scenarios. And, he said, because the Rockies were four games behind in the Wild Card race at that time, they were denied permission to print playoff tickets. As a result, tickets went on sale the day of the game.

Later, Sager noted that both teams had their bags packed for Philadelphia, where the National League Division Series that involved Game 163's winner would begin two days hence. (The Phillies won the NL East with the same 89-73 record that forced the Wild Card tiebreaker between Colorado and San Diego.) Both teams, he reported, had chartered planes, ready to leave immediately after the game; both teams had reservations at the same hotel; and both teams had scheduled a workout for 4 p.m. the next day. Only one would make the trip.

"The hotel staff in Philly is watching," Sager said. "As soon as they know who wins this game, they'll assign the rooms."

The staff in Philly would have to wait longer than usual to start assigning rooms.

The Dragon Slayer

THE GAME 163 PITCHING MATCHUP was an intriguing one, as Don Orsillo and Joe Simpson noted in their pregame comments.

"Bud Black has saved his best for last, 19-game winner Jake Peavy," Orsillo said, noting that in two starts against Colorado in 2007, Peavy had allowed only two runs in fourteen innings though he didn't get the decision in either game.

"He's in line to be a triple crown winner as a pitcher," responded Simpson, *"wins, earned run average and strikeouts. He's outstanding."*

(A slide displayed as Simpson spoke showed a 19-6 record, 2.36 ERA and 234 Ks. It was noted that if he was the winning pitcher in this game, he'd become San Diego's first 20-game winner since Gaylord Perry won 21 in 1978, the year Simpson became No. 3,000.)

Opposing Peavy, said Orsillo, was Josh Fogg.

"He loves the big stage," Simpson said. *"His teammates are calling him The Dragon Slayer. This year in matchups with aces, he's beaten Roy Oswalt, Curt Schilling, Mike Mussina and Brandon Webb. He's been good in tough games, and he'll have to be good again tonight because Jake Peavy, you don't figure to give up too many runs."*

Continuing, Simpson recapped the veteran righthander's two-sided season.

"Fogg started slowly, like some of his teammates. He was 1-5 and had an ERA just under 5 on May 17. He's gone 9-4 since."

What neither Orsillo nor Simpson knew is that the matchup of The Dragon Slayer vs. Jake Peavy had been orchestrated as much by Clint Hurdle as by Bud Black and his decision to hold Peavy out of the Sunday game against the Brewers.

"I was supposed to start Game 162," Fogg said when interviewed in 2020, "but after we won Game 161, Hurdle called me into his office and said, 'I want you to know we're going to go with Ubaldo tomorrow. We gotta win.' I think he was expecting me to put up a fight, but I was like, 'Ubaldo is throwing 99. He's been great. For sure, he should get that start. I'm perfectly fine with it.'

"Clint said, 'Alright. I'm glad you're on board. But just so you know, if we end up tying, you're starting Game 163.' I'm like, 'That's even better.' I was really excited to get the opportunity."

Fogg became The Dragon Slayer late in the 2007 season but before the start of the streak that carried the Rockies to Game 163.

"It was so weird," Josh recalled. "It was Holliday, out of nowhere. They were interviewing him after a game late in the season, and I guess I had started that game. They always ask the position players about the pitcher, and out of nowhere he dropped, 'He's our dragon slayer. He beats all the good pitchers.'

"I'd never heard of it. No one had ever mentioned anything about it before. They came over to me after, and someone said, 'Oh, I hear you're The Dragon Slayer.' I said, 'I don't know what that means.'

"They had to explain it to me, and I said, 'Oh, that's a pretty cool nickname. There could be a lot worse nicknames to have.' Holliday threw it out there, and it went from there."

Hurdle's choice to start Game 163 for the Rockies was, by then, in his seventh of nine seasons in the major leagues. A collegiate All-America at the University of Florida, Fogg was a third-round draft choice of the Chicago White Sox in 1998. Traded to Pittsburgh after appearing in 11 games for Chicago in 2001, he became one of those less expensive free agents the Rockies signed after the Hampton-Neagle debacle. He joined Colorado in 2006 and made 31 starts, finishing 11-9 with a 5.49 ERA. It was a decent return on an $850,000 investment, especially on a team with a 75-87 record that played half its games in high-altitude Denver, at spacious Coors Field.

"When I got to spring training and was meeting the guys," Fogg told *The Denver Post* years later, "you could see something building, that there was a great core group who enjoyed going on the field every day and competing." His highlight that year was facing the minimum twenty-seven batters in a two-hit, complete-game shutout against Seattle, double plays erasing the three baserunners he allowed.

One who never took himself too seriously, Fogg became one of the most popular guys in the Rockies clubhouse. "One of my all-time favorites," said his manager.

"You tell me Josh Fogg," said Game 163's improbable hero, Jamey Carroll, "I think of the teammate who allows you to come into a clubhouse and takes the stress and anxiety away because of his lighthearted character, his personality, of making you laugh, and his self-deprecating understanding of who he is. You need guys who loosen up the atmosphere, whatever the situation is. He's that way. Such a great, fun, lighthearted personality. I don't want to say he didn't take it seriously, but he knew the right time to make a joke, or his presence of saying, 'We're just playing baseball. We don't have to be so hard on ourselves.' Every clubhouse needs somebody like that."

Fogg assumed that clubhouse role during his first season in the majors.

"Knowing early on in my career that I wasn't a top-of-the-line guy—I wasn't a Number One, a Number Two or a Number Three; I was more of a back-of-the-rotation guy—I needed to bring some other things to the table besides 10 or 11 wins a year. I enjoy meeting people, enjoy talking to people. I enjoyed ... not getting into mischief but being the ringleader of things.

"With the Pirates for four years, I ran all the football pools, basketball pools and stuff like that. So, when I got to spring training in 2006, I started doing that with the Rockies. I took on the role of the guy who, if there was something going to happen, was behind it. I enjoyed setting things up with guys, whether it was dinners, t-shirts, and funny things here and there that just kept people loose and made the monotony of spring training a little bit easier. I definitely enjoyed the other aspects of baseball outside of the pitching and competing. I enjoyed the locker room and that kind of stuff.

"I enjoyed competing," he assured. "I enjoyed the competition side of sports. I loved being on the mound. I enjoyed every minute of it. I had the desire to win as much as everybody else. I just didn't feature the 98-mph fastball to go along with it. I was trying to get by with 88."

Accounts by Dan O'Dowd and one of the Rockies' coaches, Mike Gallego, of the scene that unfolded in the Rockies clubhouse after they beat Arizona to tie the Padres for the NL Wild Card capture both the camaraderie within the group and the special relationship Fogg and his teammates shared.

"After the game," O'Dowd remembered, "Clint got up in front of the club and said, 'I've got good news for you, boys. We're going to Game 163!' And the place erupted. Then he said, 'And I got bad news for you. We gotta give the ball to Josh Fogg.' And the place erupted, like, 'Oh, we got no chance.'

"Going into that game, we're matched up with Fogg against Jake Peavy. On paper, it looks like a complete mismatch. But the reality is, our team was extremely, extremely confident when Josh pitched. Because they knew that even if they got beat, they weren't going to get beat because Josh didn't compete. He had no fear. That's why they called him The Dragon Slayer. He simply did not have any fear, and that's what his teammates loved about him."

Added Gallego:

"When Hurdle announced that Josh Fogg would be our starter, all the guys in the clubhouse went, 'Oh, great. There goes our chances.' And Foggy just took it in stride. He started laughing and said, 'Hey, it isn't my fault he's putting me out there.' He knew his teammates were behind him, because there wasn't anybody else that they would have wanted out there. He

— GAME 163 —

didn't have the best stuff, but he was such a competitor. That's all these guys requested from each other. 'We're all going to make mistakes; we're all going to fail. Just don't stop competing.' That's what these guys did; they kept competing."

Their manager shared their feelings.

"He was the perfect guy for the opportunity," Hurdle said, "because he could embrace the fact he wasn't pitching against Randy Johnson or whoever, he was pitching against their lineup. And their pitcher was pitching against our guys. He never got caught up in, 'I'm facing an ace.'"

The Dragon Slayer never got caught up in the moment, either. And what a moment it was: a packed house of 48,404 on a 73-degree early evening, and every fan who couldn't get a ticket glued to a TV, following his every pitch and hanging on every word from Orsillo and Simpson.

The first batter Fogg faced in Game 163 was a former teammate. Padres right fielder Brian Giles hit 38 home runs, drove in 103 runs and batted .298 for Pittsburgh in 2002, the year Fogg joined the Pirates and went 12-12. The next season Giles' line was 16 homers, 70 RBIs and a .299 average on August 26. That's when Pittsburgh, in fourth place and going nowhere, dumped the $8.5 million salary of its second highest-paid player by trading him to San Diego (last in the NL West) for three players whose combined contracts didn't add up to a million.

Fogg's first pitch to him was low and inside. Ball One.

Giles, who had the distinction of getting the first hit in the history of Petco Park (a line single to right in the first inning April 8, 2004), was finishing his fourth full season with the Padres. His batting average was .272, with 13 homers and 50 runs batted in. A product of Dan O'Dowd's farm system in Cleveland, Giles had had the bad timing to come up with the Indians when their outfield consisted of perennial All-Stars Manny Ramirez, Kenny Lofton and Albert Belle. After fighting for playing time for four seasons in Cleveland, Giles was traded to the Pirates in November 1998, a year before O'Dowd joined the Rockies.

Despite having hit almost 150 home runs in a four-season stretch for the Pirates and reaching double figures 12 years in a row, Giles had the reputation as a disciplined hitter who made the pitcher throw strikes. A compact, muscular lefthanded swinger, Giles had led the league in walks two seasons earlier with 119 and followed that with 104 in 2006, the fifth time in his career he walked more than a hundred times. In his 15-year career, he would average 104 walks per 162 games, the length of a full season, as well as 25 home runs, 95 RBIs and a .291 batting average.

Giles swung and missed at Fogg's second offering then took another ball, making the count two balls and one strike. After taking a called strike to even the count, he grounded sharply out of Fogg's reach to second baseman Kazuo Matsui (who possessed

— GAME 163 —

one the most efficient names in baseball history—six syllables in eleven letters).

Next up was Scott Hairston, who had been a mediocre member of the NL West-winning Arizona Diamondbacks until July 27, when he was shipped to the Padres. Hairston went from hitting .222 with three homers and 16 RBIs in 76 games, to batting .288 with seven homers and 18 RBIs in 30 games. He had given San Diego just the kind of boost General Manager Kevin Towers hoped he would, and was playing for the chance to possibly show his former team that they'd given up on him too quickly. But in his first at-bat against The Dragon Slayer, Hairston struck out.

Kevin Kouzmanoff, one of two Colorado high-school products to start in the game for San Diego (the other, Josh Bard), followed Hairston. Kouzmanoff, who grew up in Newport Beach, California, moved to Evergreen (30 miles into the mountains from Denver) just before starting high school. He celebrated his 14th birthday the year Coors Field opened and rooted for the Rockies for several years. He made his major league debut as a member of the Cleveland Indians on September 2, 2006 at Texas and hit the first big league pitch he ever saw for a grand slam home run. That made him the fourth player in baseball history, dating back to 1898, to hit a slam on his first major league at-bat, and the first ever to do it on the first pitch he saw. But that apparently wasn't enough to impress the Indians; they traded him two months later to San Diego for infielder Josh Barfield. Still considered a rookie, he'd hit 18 homers and driven in 74 runs in 2007.

Fogg got ahead 0-2 but Kouzmanoff fought off the next pitch and lofted a ball to shallow right, near the foul line. Matsui, Todd Helton and right fielder Brad Hawpe converged, with Hawpe attempting a sliding catch. His divot was impressive, but the ball fell in front of him. Kouzmanoff was on with a bloop single, just his fourth hit in 20 at-bats on the Padres' critical season-ending road trip.

Not known as a strikeout pitcher, Josh Fogg had fanned only 89 in 161 2/3 innings during 2007, which was just about his average through six full seasons. But adrenaline is a funny thing. After falling behind 3-0 he struck out Adrian Gonzalez, skipping off the mound with two Ks in the first three outs.

Could The Dragon Slayer do it again?

Three runs early

"**T**he Rockies have their work cut out for them with this guy,*"* Joe Simpson said as the bottom of the first was about to begin. *"He's got electric stuff."*

But, Orsillo cautioned, *"Bud Black talked before the game: There will be some early nerves for Jake Peavy."*

The Padres' ace was only 26 years old but already in his sixth major league season. A 15th-round draft choice who proved to be one of those unexpected superstars, he'd made it to the big leagues at 21; had won the National League ERA title at 23 (2.27 and 15-6); and had been named an All-Star at 24, when he went 13-8 with a 2.88 ERA and led the National League in strikeouts with 216. In 2007 he was about to become the 12th unanimous choice ever for the Cy Young Award as the league's best pitcher (one of nine; Sandy Koufax having done it three times and Greg Maddux twice). He would pitch in the majors until he was 36 and finish with 152 victories. Late in his career he won back-to-back World Series rings as a late-season addition, first with Boston in 2013, then with San Francisco in 2014.

His career postseason record, though, didn't approach his regular-season success—one victory and five losses with a 7.98 ERA in nine games. Game 163 went similarly.

Matsui led off the bottom of the first with a liner to right center that Giles tried to cut off with a sliding stab. But the ball eluded him, and Matsui had an easy double. Troy Tulowitzki was next to the plate.

> *"Tulowitzki got off to a horrible start,"* Simpson commented, *"a guy the Rockies were counting on. But Hurdle stuck with him; he just had that look about him and the attitude: 'No worry. I'll get it going.' And, he did."*

Trying to advance Matsui to third with a shortened two-strike swing, Tulo reached safely when shortstop Khalil Greene dove to snag his bouncer up the middle but was unable to attempt a throw to first.

Next, Matt Holliday stepped into the batter's box with runners at the corners and no outs, to chants of "M-V-P . . . M-V-P" from the raucous home crowd.

After acknowledging that the most valuable player race was

between the Rockies left fielder and Philadelphia shortstop Jimmy Rollins, Orsillo said:

> *"Holliday started the season red-hot and hasn't really cooled down at any point. He's leading the league in hitting with a .340 average, three points ahead of Chipper Jones. Keep in mind, these stats count. And he's one RBI behind Ryan Howard."*

Obviously working carefully to one of baseball's most dangerous hitters that season, Peavy fell behind 3-0, causing Simpson to comment:

> *"Holliday has good numbers against Peavy, six-for-fifteen. That might be part of why Jake's trying really hard not to make a mistake here."*

After a foul ball on pitch four, Peavy missed again. Already the Rockies had the bases loaded—with Todd Helton coming to the plate. San Diego pitching coach Darren Balsley headed to the mound.

Helton, who called the last series against Arizona and the tiebreaker with San Diego "the most stressful I've ever played in," took strike one then excited everyone with a deep drive to center. But instead of a storybook grand slam, it was a sacrifice fly, caught by Brady Clark at the edge of the warning track. As Matsui trotted home with the game's first run, Tulowitzki and

Holliday both tagged up and advanced to second and third.

Garrett Atkins was next, hitting .299 with 25 home runs and 110 runs batted in.

"He has been their hottest hitter lately," said Simpson. *"He's hitting .405 over his last sixty-one games."*

Added Orsillo: *"He struggled in the beginning of the season; only .259 before the All-Star break, .345 after the break."*

With Peavy ahead 1-2, Atkins lifted a slider over short, scoring Tulowitzki. Holliday could advance only to third.

Brad Hawpe's pop to Kouzmanoff outside the third base line and Ryan Spilborghs' deep fly to right center spared Peavy further stress. But despite the quick two-run lead, Clint Hurdle wasn't overconfident.

"I managed too many games there to get too crazy," he said. "It's almost like back in the day, when you played basketball and the last bucket wins. When you play that game at Coors Field, you don't win until you've won. So, you just keep playing.

"It doesn't matter the score," he continued. "I've been underneath 10 runs; I've been on top 10 runs. Games have flip-flopped different ways.

"It takes a little pressure off you when you get off to a cleaner start. But it turned out to be a boat race, back and forth. We're up; they're up; we're up; they're up. It was good for the fans because it really energized them, charged them up, and they stayed with us throughout the night."

Buoyed by the quick two-run lead, The Dragon Slayer got Greene swinging for his third strikeout in four outs to start the top of the second. Then came the other Padre in the starting lineup who prepped in Colorado, Josh Bard.

Bard had played on consecutive state champions at Cherry Creek High School in 1995-96, during which time he'd played at Coors Field. A two-time collegiate All-America at Texas Tech, he was drafted by the Rockies in the third round in 1999. But Dealin' Dan traded him to Cleveland exactly two years later. In return the Rockies received 28-year-old outfielder-first baseman Jacob Cruz, who went to bat all of 90 times in 44 games for Colorado and managed a .211 average. As if setting an example to be followed four years hence by Kouzmanoff, Bard homered in his Indians debut—a walk-off shot against Seattle on August 23, 2002.

A catcher, Bard found himself at Coors Field October 1, 2007 because he couldn't handle Tim Wakefield's knuckleball in Boston. The Red Sox sent him to San Diego in 2006 after three passed balls in one game and four in another, all with Wakefield on the mound. (Although Bard played only seven games for Boston that season, he ended it ranked fifth in the American League with ten passed balls.) His new team, fortunately, had no knuckleballers.

Since moving to San Diego, Bard had prospered. After the trade he batted .338 in 93 games as the backup to future Hall of Famer Mike Piazza during Piazza's only season with the Padres. As the starter in 2007, he was batting a solid .283 in 117 games entering Game 163. A switch-hitter whose average was more than a hundred points higher right-on-left, Bard, swinging lefthanded, nonetheless sliced righthander Fogg's eighth delivery into left field for a clean single after fouling off five pitches. That meant the Padres' first two hits in Game 163 belonged to the two Denver-area high school products in San Diego's starting lineup—not that they were thinking about that at the moment.

"From the outside looking in, we all look from the lens of, how would this make me feel," Bard said after his playing career had long since ended. "We didn't give a lot of thought to where the game was being played. When you're in it, you're just trying to win the game with your teammates. We could have played that game on the moon, and it wouldn't have made a difference if I was from Colorado, San Diego or the moon. You're trying to beat the team in front of you."

Bard let his wife Lindsey take care of the ticket requests from family and friends. "It was nut-cutting time. I had a game plan to go over and all that," he said. "I don't know who all was there. I have no idea how many people were there." (One relative in attendance was his brother Mike, who pitched batting practice for the Rockies before home games. Josh and Mike drove to Coors Field together this day, but they avoided talking about the impending game.)

Unfazed by Bard's base hit, Fogg retired the next two hitters on four pitches. Through two innings, The Dragon Slayer had made it look easy. And his teammates were doing their part.

Seconds after Joe Simpson, opening the bottom of the second, told TBS viewers that Peavy needed to be careful with Yorvit Torrealba, Fogg's battery mate launched a 2-1 pitch deep into the left field seats for a 3-0 lead.

"I feel like I got three runs early all the time," Fogg shrugged when reliving the start of Game 163. "I was very fortunate in my career. I like to say it's because the offense knew I was going to give up runs that day. They knew it wasn't going to be 2-1 in the seventh inning. It was going to be a 5-4 game. They knew they better put their hitting shoes on whenever I was starting, because the ball was going to be put in play. They're going to score some runs, and I'm going to go out there and compete."

As everyone settled back into their seats after cheering Torrealba, a fan behind the Padres dugout won a tug-o-war for Fogg's bat after he swung at a Peavy pitch and the lumber went flying. Paid to pitch, not hit, Fogg looked at strike three. Then, retiring three hitters in a row for the first of only two times in six-plus innings of this most important start, Peavy got Matsui on a ground ball to second and Tulowitzki on his second backwards K.

The Rockies were ahead, but things were about to change.

Grand Slam

"*A game like this is like a Game Seven,*" Simpson said. "*There's no room for error. Every pitch is important; every baserunner is important. A walk, even a two-out walk, is a rally.*"

As well as, he might have said, any hit by a pitcher.

That's how San Diego's five-run third began with Peavy hitting first. A pitcher who took hitting seriously, he came into the game with a .228 batting average, four doubles, a triple and seven runs batted in.

"Unbelievable guy," Fogg said, "probably the fiercest competitor I've gotten to see on the field. Off the field, he's an unbelievable person. Just getting to share that stage with him that day was great for me. For me to be out there and get to duel with him, it was like, 'This is pretty fun.'"

After matching Fogg's bat toss into the same area of seats behind his dugout—drawing a mischievous grin from Fogg—Peavy bounced a seemingly innocent single to center, just out of the reach of a diving Tulowitzki.

"Peavy is trying to jump-start the Padres offense," Orsillo presciently remarked.

"<u>Everything</u> is a rally," Simpson reiterated. *"Again, in games like this, it doesn't matter how you get on base; just get on. Put some pressure on the pitcher. Maybe he'll make a mistake to a position player."*

Back to the top of the batting order, Fogg walked Giles on a 3-2 pitch (the first of two walks Giles would draw in the game—scoring both times), then Hairston dropped a broken-bat fly ball into right-center for a single. Quickly, the bases were loaded with no outs.

With a chance to be a hero, Kouzmanoff could manage only a fly to Holliday that left the bases loaded for Gonzalez, who was only 3-for-12 all season with three on.

Adrian Gonzalez was born in San Diego but lived in Tijuana, Mexico until he was eight years old because his father, who had played for the Mexican National Team, had an air conditioning business south of the border. Hitting .645 with 13

— GAME 163 —

home runs and 34 RBIs for Chula Vista High School in California in 2000 was enough to convince the Florida Marlins to make him the first infielder since Alex Rodriguez to be drafted No. 1 overall.

But the Marlins believed that a wrist injury Gonzalez suffered in the minors would hamper his swing long-term, so they traded him to Texas in June 2003. (He would have a 15-year career during which he hit 317 home runs, drove in 1,202 runs and compiled a lifetime batting average of .287.) After 59 largely unimpressive major league appearances during the 2004-05 seasons, he was shipped by the Rangers to the Padres as part of a five-player swap. There he blossomed in 2006, leading the team with a .304 batting average and 24 home runs. He became the first player in the history of pitcher-friendly Petco Park with multiple home runs in the same game and was voted San Diego's team most valuable player. At the start of Game 163, Gonzalez carried a .280 batting average with 29 home runs and 96 RBIS.

"He's effectively the power guy for the San Diego Padres," Orsillo had said in his opening, recapping Gonzalez's stats for 2007.

Orsillo's partner agreed, pointing out that Mike Cameron and Milton Bradley were out of the San Diego lineup with injuries. Cameron, a Gold Glove center fielder who was third on the team in home runs (21) and runs batted in (78), had suffered a partially torn ligament in his right thumb, ironically, against the Rockies in the third game of the series when Colorado swept them in San Diego a week earlier. Bradley, acquired in a late June trade, had been giving the Padres the boost they were hoping for (.313, 11-31 in 42 games) when he freakishly tore the ACL in his right knee as his manager tried to restrain him during a heated argument with umpire Mike Winters—in that same game against the Rockies.

"They really need a big night from Giles, from Gonzalez and from Khalil Greene because they've got something of a makeshift lineup," Simpson said.

Fogg had won the battle with Gonzalez in the first inning with a swinging strikeout after falling behind 3-0. But this time Gonzalez climbed on the first pitch he saw, driving it over the out-of-town scoreboard in right field.

"Sometimes pitchers try to be smarter than they need to be," Fogg reflected. "I had thrown him cutters in on his hands: cutter in, cutter in, cutter in, then changeup down and away, then back to the cutter in. And he never figured it out. He'd roll it over or swing and miss. I'd had some pretty good success."

Fogg chose Game 163, with the bases loaded, to try something different. "He hit a changeup out of the park," said The Dragon Slayer.

Game 163

"Later on, Helton comes over to me and sits down next to me in the dugout. He says, 'Hey, by the way, Gonzalez came to first base later in the game and he's like, 'I don't know why Fogg ever throws me a changeup. I can't pick up his cutter at all.' I wished I had known that a few innings earlier."

The blast was the first grand slam of Gonzalez's career, and as of 2020 still the only grand slam in tiebreaker history.

"That's not the way you draw it up," Hurdle said. "You're not thinking, 'What if he hits a grand slam?' You're thinking, 'How are we going to get him out?' You're looking for a ground ball to second, maybe a line drive at somebody, whatever."

A single by Greene, Bard's second hit—a double down the left field line—and an intentional walk to Geoff Blum loaded the bases again, with one out. The Dragon Slayer was looking pretty human at this point, but Hurdle stuck with him.

"He was the guy I wanted in that situation," he explained. "I managed by my gut all the way through that time, and I just felt he would get us where we needed to go. He would give us the innings we needed him to give us so that we could use the bullpen when we wanted to, not when we had to."

Hoping for a double play that would end the inning, Fogg coaxed a ground ball to short from Brady Clark. But Blum slid hard into second as Matsui took the throw from Tulowitzki, causing Matsui to bounce his throw to Helton at first. Greene scored from third to make it 5-3.

Still Hurdle was unconcerned. "It's kind of like, 'So what? Now what? We gotta go.' We'd been doing it for a month."

Peavy, who started the inning, batted for the second time. He made contact again, but this time Matsui caught a soft liner behind second.

The heart of the Colorado batting order awaited Peavy in the bottom of the third. Holliday grounded to second, but Helton cut the lead to one run with a first-pitch homer over the scoreboard in right. In his 10th season, all with the Rockies, Helton had played in 1,578 games, but not one in the playoffs.

"This guy wants to get to the postseason more than any other Rockie," Simpson said. *"As long as he's played, he's never been to the postseason. He's trying his best. He already has two RBIs."*

Acknowledging the near trade that would have sent Helton to Boston before the 2007 season began, Hurdle focused on why it didn't happen and what Helton's homer meant at that moment.

"He didn't want to go. He wanted to stay with the kids. He believed in this group. (His timely homer) was just another one of those things in sports you can't draw up ahead of time. It gave the team a good shot in the arm, that we were in a good place."

Peavy had allowed only 11 home runs all season, but in Game 163 he had now given up two.

It stayed 5-4 until the bottom of the fifth, but by then

GAME 163

Colorado's Dragon Slayer had departed—chased by a first-pitch, leadoff double by the man who had bludgeoned him with the grand slam in the third. It was the taciturn first baseman's 46th two-bagger of the season. Taylor Buchholz, acquired from Houston in the trade that brought Matsui from Houston, stranded Gonzalez at second with three straight outs.

"It's one thing to honor a guy by what he had done," Hurdle said of his decision to pull Fogg. "But at the same time, you have to win the game now. If you don't think he can get the next guy, he needs to come out."

Tulowitzki started the bottom of the fifth with a double just out of the reach of diving center fielder Brady Clark, and Holliday to the repeated chants of "M-V-P! M-V-P!" quickly brought him home with a rope to center, tying Philadelphia's Ryan Howard for the National League lead in runs batted in with 136, and tying the game at 5-5. The hit also restored Holliday's batting average to .340, maintaining his three-point edge on Atlanta's Chipper Jones.

> *"With that base hit he pretty much locked up the batting tile,"* Simpson said. *"The only thing that would take that away is if this game goes 20 innings."*

Jake Peavy had allowed more than four runs in a game only twice in 33 starts in 2007. Already in Game 163 he had allowed five. Clearly, he was struggling.

"You just don't know; you don't know the toll of the season," Hurdle reflected. "You don't know until you play the game. That's the beauty of it. His pitch execution might not have been what he wanted that night. But there are many nights when pitchers leave you pitches to hit, and you don't hit 'em. He gave us pitches to hit, and we hit 'em."

Despite throwing 91 pitches in his first five innings and only nine first-pitch strikes, Peavy remained the man for Bud Black.

Brady Clark began the top of the sixth with a single to center. Rather than pinch-hitting for Peavy, Black asked his ace to lay down a sacrifice bunt to move Clark to second with one out. Peavy had done it eight times during the season, so it seemed a logical move. But he stabbed and fouled twice then popped up a high, inside pitch on his third attempt. Torrealba caught it, leaving Clark at first.

Hurdle called on Jeremy Affeldt to relieve Buchholz, opting to go left-on-left against Giles. Affeldt hadn't thrown a wild pitch since O'Dowd acquired him from Kansas City before the start of the 2006 season, but in this situation he did what Peavy failed to do. Ahead 0-2, he bounced a 54-foot curve that Torrealba blocked, then threw low again. The second one went to the backstop, moving the go-ahead run into scoring position. But Affeldt did his job, getting Giles on a weak pop to short on his second, tense 3-2 pitch.

At this point, the role that Colorado's expanded September

— Game 163 —

roster played in the Rockies' run to the playoffs would be accentuated once again.

Expanded roster

It was crowded in the Colorado dugout after September 1. That's when all major-league teams were permitted to increase their active rosters above 25 players—to the maximum of 40—by recalling prospects from their minor-league affiliates and activating players from the disabled list. The approach of that eventful date filled the last week of the minor-league regular season, which ended August 31, with anticipation and apprehension for players hoping to be summoned.

"I think expectant is a good word," said Ryan Speier, whose work in relief down the stretch made him one of the most impactful callups. "You can see what kind of year you've had; you can see what kind of contribution you'll be able to make for the big club. If you had a year in Triple-A where you didn't really prove yourself, you're probably not expecting a call."

An undrafted free agent who appeared in 90 major-league games over four seasons, Speier realizes that he beat the odds.

"There's a number of factors that go into it," he said, noting the biggest one first: "How much they've invested in you. Obviously, they want to see their higher picks come up and contribute."

The players on the Sky Sox, the Rockies' Triple-A affiliate in Colorado Springs, were well aware of how things were going in Denver as their season wound to a close. Rockies games, naturally, were on the clubhouse TV.

"The Rockies put such emphasis on developing their farm system that a lot of the guys that were in the big leagues had come up with us," Speier said. "So, we're pulling hard for them and waiting for an opportunity when it presented itself for ourselves."

Deciding which players get the proverbial "cup of coffee" in September, as any brief stint with a major-league club is called, involves input from a variety of organizational minds, including the managers in the minor leagues, roving instructors, scouts, and others. But ultimately the general manager and field manager make the decisions.

"They want to have all their weapons available," Speier said. "To be able to expand their rosters in September is a big advantage for teams that have good farm systems. (In 2007, Rockies affiliates contended at every level.) They used that wisely and it paid off in September."

The number of players a team adds varies by team; the 2007 Rockies added 11.

"There are five tools," Clint Hurdle explained. "Does this guy have one tool that can help us win a game late? Is it as a pinch-hitter? As a pinch-runner? One swing of the bat and he can hit the ball out of the ballpark? Is it a lefthanded specialist out of the bullpen? Can we bring up a guy who can go right on right and get a good hitter out? Is it a defensive player who can supply the leather after you take a lead?"

The deeper bench and extra arms in the bullpen were significant factors during Colorado's final 15 games, including Game 163. Hurdle utilized 32 of the 36 players on the roster in those last two weeks—14 pitchers and 18 position players. (The other four saw action earlier in the month.) He would use 23 players in Game 163.

"You can use matchup situations early if you want to," Orsillo said in the top of the sixth. *"All of the guys who got called up are available for tonight's action."*

"I've never been a fan of September baseball," Hurdle said, "because you play it one way for five months, and it's like alley ball the last month. However, if those are the rules, we're going to play by them, and we're going to use every guy we could. I thought our organization—the guys we chose and the way they were deployed—I thought we did a fantastic job to get those guys in play and utilize the skill sets they had. We used everybody we brought up."

The contributions of the non-pitchers ranged from Clint Barmes pinch-running twice and Joe Koshansky once (oh, the luxury of burning a player just for that!) to Omar Quintanilla pinch-hitting and playing some infield in seven games, catcher Chris Iannetta getting a hit in all five games in which he played (including two home runs, one a grand slam), and Seth Smith going 5-for-6 off the bench between September 21 and October 1.

On the mound, 21-year-old Franklin Morales started three games and allowed four hits in 12 scoreless innings in the first two, and veteran Mark Redman, 33, also made three serviceable starts. Colorado won all six, with Morales the winning pitcher twice and Redman once. Hurdle called Speier from the bullpen seven times in two weeks, and the 27-year-old rookie made the most of his third chance of the season, with six scoreless outings and one hiccup, collecting three wins and one "hold." It was as if he were a different pitcher than he'd been all season.

In 50 games with the Sky Sox, Speier's record was 1-4 with a 4.38 ERA with 33 saves. In seven games with the Rockies in April and August, he had allowed 12 hits and five runs with three strikeouts. But in the streak to Game 163, Speier struck out six of the 15 batters he retired.

"I think Clint did a wonderful job of finding opportunities for each of his players where we could have the greatest likelihood of being successful," Speier said. "I think he found that with me, in being more of a matchup guy and being a guy that came in with men on base. In the minors I was mostly used as a closer.

"The big thing was we all settled into well-defined roles. I knew I was going to be matching up with Affeldt, sixth or seventh inning. We had a clearly defined closer in Corpas, a clearly defined setup man in Fuentes, and Herges as kind of a longer relief guy."

Another factor contributed to his success, Speier noted.

"Just that comfort level of knowing your job is secure at least for the month of September certainly helps," he admitted. "There's no place for them to send you. The fear of failure is still there, but it's not nearly as extreme. You have a comfort level."

With Brady Clark at second, representing the go-ahead run with two out in the top of the sixth of Game 163, Hurdle again turned to Speier. His assignment: Get Scott Hairston and preserve the 5-5 tie that Holliday's line-drive single, scoring Tulo, had produced in the bottom of the previous inning.

"I knew who I was getting and how I was going to attack him," Speier said. "That's Clint bringing us into our strength. Hairston's a guy I thought was a very favorable matchup for me—a good fastball hitter, and my strength was my off-speed."

Speier started Hairston with a fastball at 89, outside and

low, then came back with his first changeup at 80, which was fouled off. A 90-mph fastball might have caught the outside edge but was called a ball, drawing a loud reaction from Rockies fans and an exchange between Simpson and Orsillo in the TBS booth.

"Tim McClelland's not making any friends tonight," said Simpson. *"But he won't lose any sleep over it."*

"Not the first time," agreed Orsillo.

"I might have missed a call there," Speier reflected. "I thought Tim McClelland had a pretty good game, but a couple borderline pitches might have gone my way that didn't."

Another fastball at 90 was outside and low, making the count 3-1. But that meant Speier had Hairston right where he wanted him.

"Pitching behind in the count to a fastball hitter who was looking fastball," said Speier, "it kinda played to my strength to be able to get those last two pitches, even behind in the count."

Hairston fouled a slider at 80, running the count full. Before the next pitch, Torrealba trotted to the mound to make sure he and Speier were in agreement on what came next. It was another slider, at 81 mph, and Hairston swung through it. As he broke from his squat, 'Torre' pumped his fist. It was the third time Hairston had fanned in four at bats.

Speier's day was over after getting Hairston—lifted with one out in the bottom of the sixth for a pinch hitter, arguably the most impactful September callup of all, lefthanded-hitting Seth Smith.

In his fourth pro season Smith, a former college football quarterback who backed up Eli Manning at the University of Mississippi, had shown he could hit at virtually every level: Casper (.369), Modesto (.300), Tulsa (.294) and Colorado Springs in 2007 (.317). Since September 21, he'd come through with four hits in the five times Hurdle brought him off the bench to hit for someone.

Peavy started him with a pitch obviously outside then a pitch that just missed, also away. He got a called strike, down and in, then threw low. With the count in the hitter's favor, three balls and one strike, Smith lined to deep center. Clark retreated as it appeared the ball might clear the center field fence. It rebounded past Clark, requiring right fielder Giles to chase it down and throw to the infield. It was an unexpected three-base hit for Smith.

"You never know where the heroes are going to come from," Simpson said. *"That's his eighth at-bat of the year."*

'Gags'

The moment Seth Smith tripled, Mike Gallego—known by all as 'Gags'— became one of the most important figures on the field. It was a position of distinction Colorado's third base coach would assume again, seven innings later.

'Gags' was the starting second baseman on the Oakland Athletics' back-to-back-to-back American League champions of 1988-90, which meant he had experienced the rare air of the World Series, not once but three times. These were the A's of sluggers Mark McGwire and Jose Canseco, and of eventual Rockies manager Walt Weiss—all three, winners of the Rookie of the Year Award. They also were the teams of four-time 20-game winner Dave Stewart and Hall of Fame starter-turned-reliever Dennis Eckersley. The first of two pitchers in major league history to both win 20 games in a season (20-8 for Boston in 1978) and record at least 50 saves in a season (51 for Oakland in 1992), Eckersley ended a 24-year career with 197 victories and 390 saves. (The other, fellow Hall of Famer John Smoltz, won 213 and saved 154.)

But despite being favored in all three Series, Oakland won it all only once. ("We should have had three rings. We were the better team, each and every year," 'Gags' still insisted 30 years later.) The A's lost to the Dodgers in '88 in a five-game series remembered for crippled Kirk Gibson's improbable pinch home run that won Game One, his fist-pumping limp around the bases and Hall of Fame broadcaster Jack Buck's unforgettable call: "I don't believe what I just saw." The next year Oakland beat San Francisco in the even more memorable Bay Bridge Series, which became The Earthquake Series when the magnitude 6.9 Loma Prieta earthquake devastated parts of the Bay Area just before Game Three. And then they were swept by the Reds, giving Cincinnati sweeps in consecutive World Series appearances, albeit 14 years apart since the previous one came when the Big Red Machine steamrolled the Yankees in 1976.

"My attitude as a player was," explained 'Gags,' "was, if I'm going to play this game, the only way this game can be played is aggressively and fearlessly. That was the attitude of our manager, Tony LaRussa, and that was the attitude of our team: Aggressively and fearlessly. That definitely helped carry over to me as a third base coach, because, I always felt if I was going to fail, I was going to fail on the aggressive side.

GAME 163

"You knew, as a player, you had a hands-on opportunity to help win a baseball game. You knew you had an at-bat, or you knew you could make a play and make up for your at-bat, or you knew you could get a bunt down. Your heartbeat—you gotta keep your heartbeat under control in those pressure situations.

"As a coach, you didn't have anything physically that you could do. Every series, I sat for an hour or two and watched video on all the outfielders. Every team that came in, I knew. Were they good to their left? Were they quick to their right? Are they good closers? Average arm? Above-average arm? Do they throw better on fly balls? Do they throw better on ground balls? How do they move to the right? Do they turn and throw? Are they lefthanded? Righthanded?

"I watched throws that each and every outfielder made in certain situations. That's another factor. Early in the game these guys make great throws, but late in the game these throws come in offline. So, you knew these players were having a little problem with their heartbeat. They rushed themselves in tighter situations. And you couldn't get any tighter than the 13th inning against Trevor Hoffman."

What transpired at third base immediately after Seth Smith tripled in the sixth inning is most appreciated in the context of the team Smith was part of. Mike Gallego's take:

"I was proud to be a part of these guys because of how much fun they had—watching them in the clubhouse, watching them in the dugout, listening to them on the field yell and scream at each other then, as they walked off, hug each other. You talk about brotherhood and family and all that stuff. I'll be damned; this was special to watch, day in and day out. And they accepted us as coaches. They let us in; we were part of the fraternity, even though we were 20 years older. It was a great, great atmosphere to be part of. I've never—really ever—experienced anything like that, and I've been part of some close teams.

"These guys literally had fun every single day. No matter what situation they were in, no matter how bad things looked, whatever the situation was, these guys came to the ballpark every single day to have fun. It was like a Little League All-Star Team with pro players. They were ready to compete. They were ready to challenge each other. And they were going to rib each other at any moment."

That climate set the tone of the exchange 'Gags' had with Smith as the rookie picked himself up and dusted himself off, "happy as hell he made it to third," as 'Gags' put it.

"Smitty was a very intelligent young man, a good athlete. But he wasn't really fleet afoot. So, when he came sliding into third base, he popped up and looked at me and said, 'Wow! I just hit a triple. You believe that?' I said, 'No. I really don't believe that. It's amazing.'

"I said, 'Now Smitty, you're standing here on third base. I'm only going to be able to score you on a triple, because I know you're tired.' He goes, 'What? I can score on a single, can't I?' I said, 'It's going to be close.' This is the kind of ribbing we had.

"Now I'm going over the arms, because obviously they didn't pay attention in the meeting. We have a meeting before every game, and I step up and give the grades on the arms and the speed of all the outfielders. So Smitty goes, 'What are the arms like?' I said, 'Smitty, didn't you pay attention in the meeting?' He said, 'Uh, not really. Whaddya got?'

"So, I gotta go over the arms: Average arm on Clark in centerfield. Giles is average; closes well. Giles plays shallow. Clark has good speed; he's a good closer on ground balls. 'On a fly ball, be ready to get back and tag, and I'll help you out.'"

Clint Hurdle didn't interfere with his third base coach, explaining: "I don't know that it helps that much to micromanage them. I trusted Mike. He's an instinctive guy, a gutsy guy."

"Sure enough," continued 'Gags,' "he gets a short, shallow fly ball from Matsui. Smitty is going back to the bag and he's like, 'Am I going? Am I going?' I go, 'You got this, Smitty. You got this. Hell, yes. Let's go.'

"He takes off, and sure enough: One of the reports I had on Clark is he's very accurate to the bases, when he throws to second and third. But when he has a throw to home, he has a tendency to pull the ball a little bit. On this play his arm showed up pretty good because he was basically right behind second base. But he pulled it offline."

Sitting in the dugout, now a spectator, Speier was not the least bit surprised to see his friend test Clark's throwing arm.

"That was kind of always our strategy," he said. "We talked about that in nearly every coaches-players meeting before a series, that we're going to pick our spots. We didn't sit around and wait for a three-run homer very often. We put pressure on the defense: Try to take the extra base; go first to third. When we got an opportunity to get a sacrifice fly, we took it."

Thanks to Gallego's "aggressive and fearless" decision to send Smith on a not-very-deep fly, the Rockies had taken a 6-5 lead. Tulowitzki followed with a drive to center that mirrored Smith's, and he, too, wound up on third with a triple.

"Boy, are they missing Mike Cameron right now," said Orsillo. *"Brady Clark is having a tough inning in center field."*

"We talked about that early on, Don, how the Padres really missed Milton Bradley's and Mike Cameron's offense," added Simpson. *"Well, it's not going to be any more exemplified than in this inning how they miss Cameron's defense."*

Tulo's three-bagger raised hopes for another run, but Holliday struck out on three pitches—a checked swing, a hard cut and another half-swing—proving that even an MVP candidate can be overanxious in a big game. (His batting average still rounded up to .340, comfortably ahead of Chipper Jones.)

LaTroy Hawkins, who pitched in the majors until he was 43, took the mound for the Rockies in the seventh. O'Dowd had signed him to bring veteran leadership to a club that was one of the youngest in either the National or American Leagues, and he didn't disappoint.

"LaTroy turned out to be one our biggest acquisitions," Hurdle said. "The fiber, the man, the guts, the experience, the professionalism—he brought all of that to the table; to the clubhouse, to the dugout, to the bullpen. And he had it on the mound. He knew his job was to get the ball to the next guy. It was a good fit for him on our club that year, and he was a good fit for our guys."

Adrian Gonzalez reached safely with one out on a ball hit just left of second base that Tulowitzki couldn't field cleanly. In the booth Simpson thought it would be judged an error, but the official scorer called it the third hit of the day for the San Diego first baseman. Exhibiting his veteran's calm, Hawkins made sure nothing came of it. He struck out Greene and ended the inning when Bard grounded into a force at second, Matsui to Tulowitzki

One of the pivotal moments of Game 163 was soon to unfold.

Judgment call

In 2007 Major League Baseball had not yet approved Instant Replay for use in games. If it had, the Rockies might not have had to bat in the bottom of the ninth inning.

Replay is a tool that relies on umpires in New York reviewing various television camera angles of disputed plays in games being played around the country. It's intended to help the men in blue on the field get tough calls right. Utilizing 12 cameras at its inception (increased to 24 in 2020), it has been called the single biggest development for sports broadcasting since the introduction of television.

Baseball Commissioner Bud Selig, upon instituting replay on August 28, 2008, said:

> "I believe the extraordinary technology that we now have merits the use of instant replay on a very limited basis.

The system we have in place will ensure that the proper call is made on home run balls and will not cause a significant delay to the game."

Between 2008 and 2013, 387 home run calls were challenged, and 131 were reversed. Replay expanded beyond home run decisions in 2014, and unquestionably has added to the length of games. But there are far fewer mistakes; and if you believe that replay is infallible, they've been eliminated entirely. Umpires get 99.53% of all calls correct, a study in 2018 showed, and an analysis of replays then determined that 49.47% of challenged calls are overturned.

Tim Tschida was the youngest ump in the big leagues when he was promoted in 1986, and he remained so for 13 seasons. When he retired, six years after Game 163, he was only 53. Five years later, he became a part-time bartender at one of the top steakhouses in his hometown of St. Paul, Minnesota—at the invitation of the proprietor, who was his good friend. It marked his return to a job he'd enjoyed while in college and in the off seasons while he was working his way through the minor leagues.

As second base umpire in Game 163, Tschida was responsible for judging the drive Garrett Atkins hit after Todd Helton lined to Gonzalez to start the bottom of the seventh. Atkins scorched the first pitch Peavy threw him on a line toward the 390-foot sign in left center. Hairston and Clark both raced into the gap then stopped as the ball rocketed back into the field of play.

Had it cleared the fence or bounced off the very top of it? Was it a home run, or not?

Coincidentally, the same question needed to be resolved the first time a TV replay was consulted to determine the correct answer. During a game between the Florida Marlins and St. Louis Cardinals at Miami's Pro Player Stadium in 1999, outfielder Cliff Floyd of the home team hit a ball off the top of the left field scoreboard. It was first ruled a double, then changed to a home run. Then umpire Frank Pulli checked the TV monitor in the Marlins' dugout and changed it back to a double.

The Marlins, who lost 5-2, protested the use of the TV monitor. Although the National League said Pulli erred in checking the video replay and the American League agreed that replay was not to be used in the future, the protest was denied, on the basis that whether or not the ball was a home run or a double was a judgment call. Since it was not a rule violation, the call stood. It would be nine more years before Major League Baseball became the last of the four major North American pro sports to adopt a replay system.

In Game 163, Tschida said the ball hit the top of the fence and ruled it a double. Fans in the first row beyond the spot where the ball landed waved frantically and pointed to a seat back, indicating the ball had ricocheted after striking it. Hurdle charged onto the field in a futile effort to convince Tschida that he'd called it wrong. He stood, arms folded, as the umpires conferred nearby, speaking earnestly and occasionally pointing.

"The way the ball came out that hot—I've been in this park for almost 10 years, and I've never seen anything like it," he animatedly told Tschida when he finally got the chance. Gesturing to emphasize his point, Hurdle continued. "Think about it. If it hit padding, what kind of a bounce would it have? If it hits cement, if it hits iron, it's going to come back that hard, with that kind of a bounce back. So, I just don't get it. I just don't understand it.

"Can you honestly say you saw it?"

Tschida's response, Hurdle recalled, was brief and direct: "That's our call. This is what we got. This is the way we're rolling."

Hurdle begrudgingly backed off. "It didn't make sense to get thrown out. The game had too much meaning." But he didn't leave the field until he'd had a chat with home plate umpire McClelland.

"A ball can't hit the fence and have that kind of carom. That was the conversation I had with the home plate umpire. I said, 'This is a big game. You guys need to get this one right.' I said, 'This could have consequences.' I don't think that played out later in the game, but we had a nice conversation. You see it now, there's no doubt in my mind. It was a home run."

The TBS crew sided with the umpire.

"*That appears to hit the yellow line,*" Simpson said as he studied the TV replay. "*It has to clear that.*"

"*Very difficult to tell,*" Orsillo agreed.

"*I didn't see it clear the yellow line,*" Simpson reiterated. "*I saw that man standing there with the glove, trying to catch it. It didn't look like the ball came over the fence where he could reach over the chair and try to catch it.*"

"*It has to be conclusive,*" Orsillo said.

Craig Sager eventually made his way to the fans in left center, who, of course, insisted it was a home run. He introduced Inez Selby, standing next to him, and said, "Nobody had a better view." Selby, Sager reported, "claims the ball cleared the yellow padding, hit the railing behind it and bounced back onto the field." Then, in Sager's inimitable style, he added: "She's convinced. But, of course, she could be a little biased. She's a season ticketholder for the last fourteen years!" (Which covered the entire existence of the Colorado Rockies franchise.)

Tschida's call stood: a two-base hit. Unbelievably, it was the fourth time that season an apparent home run hit by a Rockies player had been ruled a double: Atkins in Cincinnati, Tulowitzki in St. Louis on the same road trip, and Torrealba in Philadelphia (nullifying a grand slam). Up in the general manager's suite, Dan O'Dowd just shook his head.

"I'd had so many bizarre calls in that ballpark over the years, things that just did not make sense at all to me, that I almost got to a point where I got numb about it." Reflecting on the historic nature of what he witnessed that night, he added: "I do think that game—again, looking at the 30,000-foot view—that game really was an impetus to move the whole replay discussion along. That winter, the replay discussion was front and center in every meeting I went to."

Pinch-runner Jamey Carroll took Atkins' place at second, a move O'Dowd questioned at the time. "There's always that question in our ballpark: Should you ever pinch-run for one of your better bats? Because you need to score as many runs as you can, but you need to create as much distance in those runs as you possibly can. When Jamey pinch-ran for Atkins, I was like, 'Aaayy?'"

Carroll and Padres second baseman Geoff Blum, teammates on their way to the big leagues, exchanged pleasantries. "We had won a championship together in Double-A," Carroll said. "So, I had known him for a long time. I'm sure I said something to him like, 'This is what it's all about.' Maybe some trash talking in a good way."

Peavy's day ended after he issued an intentional walk to Brad Hawpe. He had thrown 118 pitches with one out in the seventh inning, a determined but beleaguered effort.

The new pitcher was burly Heath Bell, who entered the

game in a double-switch that saw Michael Barrett replace Bard behind the plate—a change that would be more noteworthy a couple hours later. "This is what I gotta do," Black told Bard. "We gotta try to win."

Nonetheless, "I was pissed," Bard said of being replaced—not that it didn't happen several times in his career. "It's a part of the gig; part of being part of the team. I was just pissed that it was me. I knew what Heath Bell meant to us, as far as him being able to pitch multiple innings. I got that piece."

In his first season with San Diego after three unremarkable years with the New York Mets, Bell had struck out 97 batters in 91 innings and had compiled a 2.08 earned run average.

"I knew when Heath Bell came into the game that we weren't going to hit," O'Dowd said. "We never hit that guy. We never touched that guy."

Bell overpowered Spilborghs and Torrealba in eleven pitches, fanning both. Instead of the Rockies leading by two, it remained a one-run game going to an eventful top of the eighth.

Miscue

During his preface to the TBS telecast of Game 163, Joe Simpson noted that the Rockies were the best defensive team in the major leagues in 2007. He later noted they'd committed only 67 errors in 162 games—twelve fewer than second-place Baltimore, the American League leader. It was a major reason why Colorado was contending for a playoff berth, he said.

> *"Defense is something these Rockies do better than anyone in the National League,"* Orsillo agreed. *"They have been fantastic. It's something that Clint Hurdle talked about today before the game. They took it very seriously a long time ago, and this team's defense is what they pride themselves on."*

The team's defense wasn't only the best in the majors in 2007, it was the best EVER—the .98925 fielding percentage setting a record. And, amazingly, it was achieved without a Gold Glove defender at any position. Both Todd Helton and Troy Tulowitzki had better fielding percentages, more total chances, better zone ratings, better range factors and more assists—and turned more double plays—than those who were voted the best defensive players at their positions. Helton committed only two errors all season, compared with seven by the Cubs' Derek Lee, the choice at first base. And Tulowitzki, he of the unassisted triple play, had the same number of errors as the winner, Jimmy Rollins of the Phillies, but did it in 117 more chances (834 to 717). Somehow, though, all of that wasn't enough.

But those slights didn't diminish the pride Head Groundskeeper Mark Razum and his team felt in helping the players achieve such fielding excellence. Painted on the wall of the Ground Crew's quarters located off the tunnel in the corner beyond the left field fence is a likeness of a playing field. Attesting to the achievement, words printed within the image of the field read:

MAJOR LEAGUE HISTORY

In 2007 the Colorado Rockies established a major league record for the highest team fielding percentage of .989 and committed the fewest errors ever with 68. (No. 68 came in the 11th inning of Game 163.)

"He was a big part of the year we won our league and went to the World Series," Hurdle said of Razum years later. "He was as much a part of the team as anyone." Of Razum's crew, Hurdle added: "They are good. They are efficient. It's almost like watching a pit crew at a motorsports race . . ."

Razum grew up in Cleveland and was a classmate of former Ohio State All-American and NBA number one draft choice Clark Kellogg, the eventual CBS television basketball analyst. He worked for the head groundskeeper at Cleveland Municipal Stadium while he was still in high school. The baseball Indians shared the playing field with the football Browns, which exposed Razum to his first big groundskeeping challenge. He came to Denver the year before Coors Field opened, which meant he was, so to speak, with his field from the ground up. Before that, he had tended the field at Oakland-Alameda County Coliseum, another site shared by baseball (Athletics) and football (Raiders). There his field was voted the best in the American League three straight years.

There had been no unusual defensive plays through the first seven innings of Game 163, but that changed in the top of the eighth. Oddly, there was nothing Razum or his workers could have done to prevent it, and nothing they did contributed to it.

Jamey Carroll took over at third base after running for Atkins, batting fifth behind Holliday and Helton, and Hurdle brought reliever Brian Fuentes into the game, replacing

Hawkins. But with an eye toward the batting order in the bottom of the eighth, he put him in Spilborghs' seventh spot, which was the next-to-last at-bat in the inning just concluded. Cory Sullivan went in to play center field in place of Spilborghs, slotted to lead off the home half of the eighth from the pitcher's normal ninth spot in the batting order.

Fuentes had been the closer for much of the 2007 season, but a disastrous road trip to Toronto, Wrigley Field in Chicago then Houston between June 22 and July 1 relegated him to eighth-inning set-up man behind Manny Corpas for the rest of the year. During that 10-game trip, Fuentes blew four consecutive save opportunities—all walk-off defeats. The Elias Sports Bureau, keeper of baseball's voluminous (and often obscure) records, determined that Fuentes was the first relief pitcher since "Saves" became a statistic to blow four in a row.

Fuentes pitched well after a short stint on the disabled list, holding opponents to a .159 batting average and allowing only four earned runs in 24 games (a 1.52 ERA). But Corpas went 16-for-16 in save opportunities after taking over for Fuentes and kept the closer's job despite his teammate's return to form.

"That made us even better," O'Dowd said, "because now Clint could deploy him in an earlier inning, which made our bullpen that much deeper."

What happened to Fuentes in the eighth inning of Game 163 was a microcosm of his checkered season. After allowing a leadoff

— GAME 163 —

single to Geoff Blum, Fuentes retired Brady Clark on a pop foul to Helton. Then Michael Barrett, who replaced Josh Bard behind the plate when Heath Bell replaced Peavy, struck out on a wild pitch that allowed Blum to move into scoring position.

Brian Giles—3-for-24 in his career against Fuentes—took his first pitch for a ball, low and away, then swung and missed badly at a breaking ball in almost the same place. It appeared Fuentes had pitched his way out of the inning when Giles fought off the next pitch and lofted a fly ball toward Matt Holliday in left. But the Rockies' record-breaking defense was about to betray its erstwhile closer.

Holliday hadn't exactly been a Gold Glove candidate during his first three seasons. But after 20 errors in 436 games (a fielding percentage of .972), he had committed only three in 156 games in 2007 (a career-high .990). That he wasn't charged with his fourth E-7 on Giles' high, arching drive is only because he never got a glove on it.

By the time Holliday realized that breaking IN on the ball was a mistake, it was over his head. Giles coasted into second with a run-scoring double, Blum's run tying the game at 6-6. Fuentes was charged with another blown save.

"I thought Giles got jammed a bit on that," Speier said from Tulsa, where he lives in retirement. "I wasn't surprised Matty misplayed that one. The ball carries in funny ways every now and then at Coors Field."

Expressing the feelings of virtually all of Holliday's teammates, Speier added: "Matty was solid for us all season. In my eyes, he was the MVP—for us, certainly, if not the league. Making a miscue; it comes with the territory. It's going to happen. I think he made up for it later."

"We've seen some less-than-stellar outfield play tonight," Simpson said to Orsillo. *"That quieted this crowd; what looked like a routine fly ball turned into anything but. A horrible time for a misplay . . . a gift from what has been a good defensive ball club."*

"As soon as he took the step in, I knew he was screwed," said O'Dowd, who was philosophical about the misplay. "That's just part of it. That was the ebb and flow of that game."

Declaring, "We ripped the rearview mirror off our car long before that," Hurdle viewed it similarly. "Matty played such a good outfield for us all season long. It was just one of those things. Again, it was, 'So what? Now what?' At that point in time, let's move on."

Move on, the Rockies did. And Holliday, as Speier put it, made up for his goof.

"Had we not won," Holliday later said, "I probably would have had nightmares all winter. I took a bad step, missed the ball."

Three innings

Heath Bell walked Cory Sullivan leading off the eighth, and Brad Hawpe with two outs in the ninth, but he was unhittable. Corpas pitched a 1-2-3 ninth in between.

"In the history of tiebreakers, there's only been one, one-run game," Simpson said as a TBS camera picked up a fan in the stands holding a sign that read, "IT COULD HAPPEN."

"We're headed for extra frames," Orsillo said, *"tied at six."*

The 10th through the 12th saw anxious moments, but Matt Herges for the Rockies and San Diego's Joe Thatcher—who had allowed the game-losing hits by Brad Hawpe and Vinny Rottino in the previous nine days—worked through the tension.

Originally a member of the Los Angeles Dodgers, Herges was a rookie at age 30 in 2000. By 2003 he was with San Diego and appeared in 40 games for the Padres, with a 2-2 record and a 2.86 ERA, before he was traded to San Francisco in mid-season. With the Giants that year, he appeared in 27 games and had a 1-0 record and 2.31 ERA. Traded by the Giants June 3, 2005, he made seven relief appearances for Arizona, then was waived. The Marlins signed him for the 2006 season.

The next year, at 37, he became the second player in history to play for all five National League West Division teams when he joined Colorado on February 18, 2007. He pitched unimpressively in two April games and was sent outright (not optioned) to Colorado Springs. The Rockies purchased his contract July 3 after he posted a 1.27 ERA in 32 games in Triple-A, and he went 5-1 with a 2.74 ERA in 32 games from the Fourth of July through Game 162. Then he made a huge contribution in Game 163.

Herges equaled his longest outing of the season against the Padres in Game 163, though this time was significantly different. When he pitched the sixth through the eighth on August 8 against Milwaukee, the Rockies were cruising, 16-3, on their way to a 19-4 victory. That day he threw only 30 (pressure-free) pitches. On October 1 he worked the 10th through the 12th of a 6-6 tie with the postseason at stake and threw 47 pitches— his most, by 13, of any game that season.

GAME 163

In the 10th, he walked pinch-hitter Termel Sledge with two outs then gave up a single to Bard's replacement, Michael Barrett. But Giles grounded a 2-2 pitch sharply to Tulowitzki, who turned it into a force at second.

"I think Giles hit a pretty hittable pitch," Herges admitted. "I may have missed my spot. He hit it pretty firmly, but he didn't get any lift on it. I'm walking off the mound, going, 'That's super exciting, but, omigosh, I just got away with something here.'"

The 11th began with Carroll, guarding the third base line, preventing a double by Hairston. But he pulled Helton off first with a wide throw for the Rockies' 68th error of the record-setting season.

"My job at that point in time," Carroll recalled, "was to supposedly be better at defense than Garrett Atkins. It's something I prided myself on my whole career, my defense. What went through my mind then was that I'd just made the inning more stressful for our pitcher. You have to move on from it and hope you get another opportunity to make up for it."

And that's exactly what happened. After a sacrifice bunt by Kouzmanoff, Adrian Gonzalez was intentionally walked, putting two on with one out. For the second inning in a row—anticipating the Padres taking the lead—Trevor Hoffman began warming up. But again, Herges escaped, this time by inducing Greene to hit a ground ball to Carroll, who stepped on third then threw to Helton, on target this time, to complete the double play. Coors Field erupted.

"At that moment," Herges recalled, "walking off the mound, I literally felt my hair shake. That's how loud it was. I've never felt that anywhere else. It literally erupted and I felt my hair shake. The whole bank of people was screaming at the field."

"There was a picture of me running off the field right after that," said Carroll, "and you can see the crowd in the background. For me, that's a prideful picture. I have it on my wall at home. It's a shot of me in my career overcoming something and doing something to put a team in a special situation."

In the Rockies dugout a silent scene played out in the bottom of the 11th inning. Pitching coach Bob Apodaca approached Herges and gave him a hand gesture that told Herges he'd be going out for a third inning if the Rockies didn't win it on the spot.

"To myself," said Herges, "I'm thinking, 'I don't know what's going to happen here.' So, I sit down like I'm still locked in. 'Dack' walked over and looked at me, put his hands together and made a 'one,' like, 'One more?' The feeling I got was, 'We need you to go back out.' I couldn't remember the last time I'd pitched three innings, but I'm sure he knew I'd done it previously that season. 'Absolutely,' I said."

The third Coloradan on San Diego's active roster, relief pitcher Doug Brocail, from Lamar, had worked a perfect 10th and got the first two outs in the 11th before he walked Helton and allowed a line drive single to right by Carroll. Bud Black decided it was time for a rematch: Thatcher versus Hawpe, with the season on the line.

An all-region player who once set the school record for three-pointers in a game for Kokomo High in basketball-crazy Indiana, Thatcher was in his first year of a nine-year major league career in 2007. He entered Game 163 with a 1.37 ERA and a .176 batting average-against. He would develop into a very effective "situational" lefthanded reliever, meaning he was good at getting out the other team's lefthanded batters late in games.

Against Hawpe on this occasion, he got ahead quickly as Hawpe swung mightily and missed on successive pitches. After two pitches that were intentionally high in hopes Hawpe would chase, Thatcher came back with another in the strike zone that Hawpe again whiffed at.

* * *

The 12th, began with Herges walking Morgan Ensberg, a double-switch replacement. Another sacrifice bunt followed. Then came a pinch-hitter Herges was seeing for the first time. Brian Myrow had been called up in September after winning the Pacific Coast League batting title with a .354 average for Portland. It prompted a visit to the mound by Apodaca and catcher Torrealba.

"I didn't know him," Herges admitted. "And that's no excuse.

I should have known everybody who potentially could come into the box. What I did know is that he was a late callup. So, he's pretty anxious. He has more pressure on him than I do on myself."

As home plate umpire Tim McClelland gently prodded Apodaca to wrap up his conference and the coach withdrew, Torrealba lingered briefly.

"He was about as prepared, creative, confident as any catcher I've ever had," Herges said. "I was fortunate to have a high amount of great people who caught me. But 'Torre' was, by far, the best prepared, most creative—he would just make you believe in yourself."

On the TBS telecast, Joe Simpson commented:

> *"We know he was well-schooled in the dugout by the veteran hitters what to expect from Herges . . . It's hard to be patient in this situation when you're a young guy like Myrow, trying to do something special for your team and your city."*

Herges started him with a breaking ball outside. His second pitch was on the outside corner, called strike one. After another outside pitch made it 2-1, Myrow swung at a changeup that was down and away; 2-2. He swung again and missed on another changeup in the same location. Two out.

"A veteran handling a rookie, there," said Simpson.

That brought Herges' good friend and former teammate, Michael Barrett, to the plate; a runner at second, still, and, now, two out. Barrett already had one hit against him, a single in the 10th.

"Michael and I played together in Montreal in '02," Herges said, "and we had apartments right next to each other. His wife and my wife got really close. We didn't room together, but we were always in the same place. We went to dinner together a lot. I had a heightened sense of, 'I have to get this guy.'"

After Herges fell behind 3-0 and Barrett took a called strike, the cat-and-mouse game began. Herges peered at Torrealba. Barrett stepped out. Herges went with his changeup, and Barrett lined it wide of the third base and into the seats. He muttered to himself about missing a hittable pitch. Torrealba made another mound visit, then Barrett again stepped out of the batter's box.

Finally, Herges made his 47th and final pitch, another changeup. Barrett broke his bat and grounded slowly to Tulowitzki, who charged and threw him out on the run.

"I was pitching him away, away, away," Herges recalled, "and I missed my spot and got really fortunate because it jammed him. I remember him giving me that look, running down to first, like, 'Are you kidding me? YOU know, and I know, you didn't mean to put that pitch there. I was hanging out over the plate, and you missed your spot and got lucky.'"

Herges had thrown more balls (24) than strikes (23) but remained calm throughout, which didn't surprise O'Dowd.

"That was Matty," O'Dowd said. "He had a slow heartbeat. He never panicked. He knew how to execute a pitch when he needed to execute a pitch. To me, when we talk about that game, in my mind if you look at all the guys that threw that night, he's the reason we won that game. He's the reason."

A place in history

After Thatcher retired the Rockies in order in the 12th, Hurdle turned to Jorge Julio to succeed Herges in the top of the 13th inning. Although his record was 0-3, he had a 3.59 ERA, and in 52 2/3 innings had allowed only 48 hits. With seven bullpen arms already called into the game, Julio seemed the best available option.

Julio had come to the Rockies from the Marlins, in exchange for South Korean eccentric Byung-Hyun Kim, on May 13. As Baltimore's hard-throwing closer in 2002, Julio had finished with 25 saves and a 1.99 ERA, and placed third in Rookie of the Year voting. During the next two seasons he saved 36 and 22, but his ERA climbed, to 4.38 in 2003 and 4.57 in 2004. After a stellar April in 2005, his performance nose-dived. He was traded to the New York Mets in January 2006, beginning a nomadic journey through Arizona and Florida before he landed in Colorado in May 2007.

Julio's 13th began with a five-pitch walk to Giles, then got worse. His first pitch to Hairston was a ball, and his second, a 94-mile-per-hour fastball, landed in the seats in left-center—about fifteen feet to the right of the spot where Atkins' drive landed. As he jogged past Jamey Carroll and headed for home plate, the usual congratulatory handshake from the third base coach came from Glenn Hoffman, Trevor Hoffman's older brother, who was in his second season with the Padres in that role.

"I felt like the whole stadium felt," Carroll said. "The air was let out of you. It was such a game—we were going back and forth, and you're getting in these later innings where people are working out of jams . . . people don't have much going . . . and all of a sudden, like a quick jolt in the other direction. 'Oh boy, where do we go from here?' Knowing Trevor Hoffman was going to be coming in, it was going to be a fight. First emotion is, 'Oh, no, this could be over. Everything we'd gone through, the run we had made. It goes through your mind: 'This could be it.' Fortunately, we still had the opportunity left to hit."

In the dugout, Ryan Speier was thinking it might be over. "At that point, I was re-evaluating the season and thinking, 'Man, it can't end like this.'"

Up in his box, O'Dowd was not feeling good, either. "I really loved Kevin Towers (the late San Diego GM), and Buddy

Black and I had worked together for years in Cleveland. And Paul Podesta was there, and he and I had worked together for years. In my mind, I'm trying to think, 'What can I say to these guys that is going to sound authentic?'"

At least one member of the Padres, starting catcher Josh Bard, who was replaced by Michael Barrett in the double-switch that brought Heath Bell into the game in the seventh inning, didn't see Hairston's go-ahead blast.

"I'd been playing with a torn (tendon) in my wrist for about a month and a half," Bard said, "so as soon as they took me out, I went up and was going to get a cortisone injection if we won the game. I was actually in the training room when he hit the home run, literally sitting with the doctor, waiting for an injection if we won."

Yet another player with Colorado ties, Chase Headley from Fountain (there were four, plus the bullpen coach, the late Darrel Akerfelds, who played at Columbine High in metro Denver), batted for Thatcher. Headley lined the third pitch he saw to right for a single. Three batters, ten pitches, two hits, two runs and a runner on base. Hurdle couldn't afford to let Julio face the next batter—Adrian Gonzalez, who already was 3-for-5 and needed a triple to hit for the cycle.

Ramon Ortiz was the next man up in the Rockies bullpen, completing the ninth of what would be a 12-year major league career spread over 15 seasons. Exclusively a starter the first eight years in the big leagues (with an 82-80 record), the 34-year-old righthander was being used in relief by Clint Hurdle. And the results hadn't been very good. In nine games Ortiz had allowed 15 hits and 11 runs in 12 innings—an ERA of 8.25. It had been 15 days since Hurdle called him into a game—the last time on September 15 in a 10-2 loss, the day before the streak to Game 163 began. But rusty or not, he had the most experience of the remaining relievers.

"There's always that concern," Hurdle conceded. "What's he going to do. But he'd been pitching since he was six years old. I felt he was the best option at the time. I told him: 'Stop them right here, and we'll win this game.' Sometimes you say that half-heartedly, but this was a big stop for us. He came in and did it."

Entering the game in the 13th inning with Headley on first base and already trailing by two runs, Ortiz found a familiar face awaiting his first pitch: Gonzalez, the hitting star of the game for San Diego. Three years earlier, with Ortiz on the mound for the Angels on April 20, 2004, Gonzalez recorded his first major league hit, a single.

Ortiz worked Gonzalez away. Ball One was high and outside, then Gonzalez swung and missed. The third pitch was in the same location as the first, then Gonzalez swung and fouled. Pitch five sailed outside, then Gonzalez swung and missed again—six pitches, one out.

Ortiz needed only four more pitches to end the inning with a fly to left field that Holliday gathered in at the warning track and a pop that Tulowitzki caught in shallow center.

"I don't think anyone was thinking, 'Oh, no! Here comes Ramon,'" said Matt Herges. "It was, 'Ramon's going to get us out of it.' And he did it.

"It could have gotten really ugly, real quick. But Ramon came in, and not only did he stop the bleeding, he shut it down—totally got out of it. For me, he was the hero. What Ramon did in the 13th inning gave us hope. Once you heard the crack of Hairston's bat, you knew it was gone. It was so deflating. And then Ramon comes in and shuts it down and gets us back in the dugout. I don't think enough can be said for the job he did."

Julio was in line to be the losing pitcher, but if the Rockies could rally one more time, Ortiz could have his first victory as a member of the Rockies—a historic one, at that.

It would prove to be Ortiz's only for Colorado. He left as a free agent after the season and signed with San Francisco, the first of eight subsequent stops before injury ended his major-league career. Hanging on until he was 40 years old, the skinny Dominican bounced among seven major-league teams (the Giants twice) the next six seasons and appeared in 45 major-league games. He also played in Japan and for six minor league teams from coast to coast (Buffalo twice). He injured his arm June 2,

2013 when throwing a pitch for Toronto in the third inning of a game against—of all teams—the San Diego Padres. He played two more years in the Mexican and Dominican Winter leagues but never appeared in another MLB game.

"Hells Bells"

GONG...... GONG...... GONG......
GONG...... GONG...... GONG......

The heavy-metal song that begins this way is called "Hells Bells," and from 1998 to 2010, whenever San Diego Padres fans heard that sound, they knew it was time for opposing batters to face the music. Trevor Hoffman, the best closer of his generation and one of the greatest of all time, was on his way to the mound.

"'Hells Bells' in San Diego IS Trevor," an opponent once said with a mixture of respect and awe. "It's like when you go there, you want to win, but only two out of three, so you can hear it once."

The lyrics were barely, if ever, heard before Hoffman reached the mound and the sound system relented—overwhelmed by the blaring electric guitars, pounding drums and crashing cymbals and finally, the throbbing bass, generated by the Australian hard-rock group AC/DC. But the words that followed were prophetic, nonetheless.

The first verse begins:

I'm a rolling thunder, a pouring rain
I'm comin' on like a hurricane . . .

And the opening line of second goes:

I won't take no prisoners,

Initially, the hometown newspaper, *the Union-Tribune*, called Hoffman's entrance song "more suited to the World Wrestling Federation than the national pastime."

But it caught on in a big way, as Tom Verducci once wrote in *Sports Illustrated*:

"His signature moment is one of the most electrically charged in sports: Padres fans rising and roaring, in Pavlovian fashion, upon hearing the first bell toll, the foreboding bonging like something out of Hitchcock as Hoffman enters slowly, stage right."

"Hells Bells" was released on October 31, 1980—nineteen days after Trevor Hoffman's thirteenth birthday. Back then, no one imagined it would one day become the death knell for Major League Baseball teams hoping to rally to victory in the ninth inning of games, first at Jack Murphy Stadium and, later, at Petco Park.

Trevor Hoffman was a 5-foot-6, 130-pound freshman shortstop at Savannah High in Anaheim in 1980—a shortstop because his protective father Ed didn't trust the prep coaches with his son's arm. From age 12 to age 24, Trevor didn't throw a single pitch.

Ed Hoffman was an ex-Marine, a veteran of bloody Iwo Jima in World War II. He was a touring professional singer until he tired of being away from his family and became a postal worker. He ushered at Angels games—leading fans in "Take Me Out To The Ball Game" and occasionally singing the national anthem, usually when the scheduled singer didn't make it. Ed often brought Trevor and Trevor's mom Mikki with him to see the Angels play. Mikki had been a ballerina in her native Great Britain, her father a professional soccer player before the war.

Growing up, Hoffman couldn't follow in the sometimes-choppy footsteps of his soccer-playing grandfather. He couldn't play football, either. Even wrestling was out of the question. When he was an infant, only six weeks old, one of his kidneys was removed because it was creating an arterial blockage. So, Trevor concentrated on baseball. And once he became a star, he gave back. For every save, he contributed $200 to the Southern California chapter of the National Kidney Foundation, and at each Saturday home game he hosted a group of children with kidney-related illnesses.

Although his brother Glenn, nine years older, was the starting shortstop for the Boston Red Sox, and despite Trevor starring on his high school team, no college baseball coach offered him a scholarship when he graduated from Savannah High. So, he walked on at Cypress College, a junior college in Anaheim. A year later he was recruited to the University of Arizona, and in 1988, his senior season, he led the team with a .318 batting average and caught the eyes of scouts with his strong arm at short.

The Cincinnati Reds drafted him as a shortstop in the 11th round of the 1988 amateur draft (289th overall) and signed him for $3,000. But after hitting .249 in sixty-one games at Rookie League Billings and .211 in 103 games at Charleston in the Class A South Atlantic (Sally) League the next season, Hoffman became a pitcher. Bluntly, a Reds scout told him he was a mediocre hitter but his ability to throw 95 mph could get him a job as a pitcher in the big leagues. (In 18 major-league seasons his earned run average would be 3.08, while his lifetime batting average was .118.)

Hoffman spent the 1991 and 1992 seasons converting from infielder to pitcher. At Cedar Rapids, Chattanooga and Nashville combined, he won nine and lost seven, with a 2.90 ERA and, most impressive, 169 strikeouts in 142 2/3 innings pitched.

— GAME 163 —

Available in the 1992 expansion draft, when the Colorado Rockies and Florida Marlins were stocked to begin play in 1993, Hoffman was the eighth player chosen (fourth round, by Florida). "We had him as the highest-rated player in their system," Dave Dombrowski, then-Marlins general manager, once said. "When you look back over all the expansion drafts in history, Trevor is probably the best player ever taken who wasn't already an established big leaguer."

Pitching for a team that wound up losing ninety-eight games in its first year of existence, Hoffman posted a 2-2 record and 3.28 ERA in twenty-eight appearances through June 23, 1993. But lured by the prospect of adding a budding star in 24-year-old Gary Sheffield, the Marlins traded Hoffman away. Sheffield, who had won the National League batting title in 1992, would be a seven-time all-star and have a career almost as long as Hoffman's. But he would leave the Marlins six years later, while Hoffman starred in San Diego for 16 seasons.

Hoffman was actually booed on occasion his first season in San Diego. He gave up three runs in one inning in his Padres debut and allowed eight runs in his first three appearances. He even blew his first save opportunity. Appearing in 39 games for a team that lost 101 times, he finished that first season with a 2-4 record and a 4.38 ERA—the only time with the Padres that his ERA was over 4.00. (It was under 3.00 in all but two of the other fifteen seasons.)

The strike by the Major League Players Association in mid-1994 not only cut in half Hoffman's first full season with the Padres and wiped out the World Series that year, but it also indirectly forced him to become a different, and ultimately better, pitcher. The day after the strike began, Hoffman went to a beach in Del Mar, 22 miles up the coast from San Diego, with some guys he grew up with. They played beach volleyball and tossed a Nerf football. While playing volleyball, Hoffman lunged for a shot that had been dinked over the net. When he landed in the sand, he felt a sharp pain in his shoulder. Later, while playing catch in the ocean, Hoffman dove for a ball. He thought he was in fairly deep water but landed on a sandbar. Again, he felt a sharp pain in his shoulder.

When the strike finally ended and the 1995 season started—in late April—Hoffman's blazing fastball was no more. He eventually had surgery.

He'd worked on a changeup, but it was nowhere near the dominant pitch he became known for. Then a fellow reliever named Donnie Elliott taught him a new grip for his changeup. It is Elliott's sole claim to fame as a baseball player. He appeared in 30 games in 1994 and once in 1995. His career line for 31 games is an 0-1 record and 3.27 earned run average. Meanwhile, relying on the changeup Elliott taught him, Trevor Hoffman became the first closer in baseball history to record 500, then 600, saves.

Hoffman was admired by his peers for his ability to succeed at such a high level without the high-velocity fastball that initially had made him such a promising pitching prospect. The best relievers at the time doubted that they themselves could have reinvented themselves the way Hoffman did. And hitters almost dreaded having to face him.

"Some guys overpower you; Hoffman embarrasses you," said former opponent and one-time teammate Mike Piazza.

"It's like it has a parachute on it," said Paul Lo Duca, who came up with the Dodgers the year Piazza left Los Angeles, after striking out on Hoffman's vaunted changeup.

Hoffman converted almost 89 percent of his "save opportunities" and set a record (later broken by Mariano Rivera) with 601 saves. When he retired after the 2013 season, he held the Major League Baseball records for 20-save seasons (15), 30-save seasons (14, including eight straight), and 40-save seasons (9, including four in a row twice). He was enshrined in the Baseball Hall of Fame at Cooperstown in 2018.

During his HOF acceptance speech, Hoffman quoted legendary college basketball coach John Wooden several times. One quote, in particular, described what Hoffman called "an amazing journey." It went, "Things turn out best for those who make the best of how things turn out."

As the bottom the 13th inning of Game 163 was about to begin at Coors Field, there were no "Gongs" to be heard. The stadium had been quieted noticeably by Scott Hairston's two-run homer in the top of the inning. Everyone knew, and dreaded the thought, that the time had come for the future Hall of Famer with one kidney to bring it home for the Padres.

"This is reality."

Before Game 163, Trevor Hoffman had faced the Rockies five times during the 2007 season. In those five games he came away with a victory and three saves (Nos. 28, 30 and 37 in a season of 42), and faced the minimum 15 batters in five innings, allowing one hit (to Todd Helton) but erasing him on a 5-4-3 double play off the bat of the next hitter, Matt Holliday. He had needed only 61 pitches, an average of 12 per appearance.

Understandably, Rockies fans were not optimistic as he strode to the mound. 'Gags' felt it on his way to the third base coaching box.

"The only people you could hear talking were the Padres in their dugout. The stands were completely silent. It was unbelievable. As loud as it had been all day, there was nothing. I'm running out and I can hear my cleats crunching in the dirt. I'm thinking, 'Man, that was a great run we had.'

"Are you kidding me? Trevor Hoffman has HOF in his name. This guy is the best in the game, and we hadn't had much success against him over the years. We knew this is what the Padres were hoping to get to. They were hoping for a one-run lead—let alone a two-run lead. It was over."

Despite the odds, O'Dowd still thought there was a chance.

"I had this feeling inside that if somehow we could get a couple guys on base . . . I knew Trevor was coming into the game, but I didn't think Trevor was as dominant in our ballpark as he was in other places. And it kinda worked out that way."

Down in the dugout, hitting coach Alan Cockrell approached Hurdle with a question. "Do you want us to take a strike?"

"It's one of the conversations you have," said Hurdle, "Take a strike or just let 'em rip? I said, 'This guy's hard enough to hit with three strikes. I don't want to send our guys up with just two. Be ready to hit. Let's go.'"

Cockrell relayed the word: "Be ready to hit."

Hoffman was facing the first two hitters in the inning for the first time in 2007. Kaz Matsui had gone 0-for-3 against him while with the Mets after coming from Japan in 2004, and Tulowitzki had struck out in his only at-bat against the wicked changeup the previous September.

Matsui fell behind then evened the count at two balls and two strikes. On the sixth pitch he saw from Hoffman, he doubled to deep right-center.

"Kaz had the ability to rise to the occasion," O'Dowd said. "Him getting that inning going the way he did really set the tone for the 13th."

Tulowitzki went to a full count, fouled the next pitch, then doubled to left center, scoring Matsui.

Two batters, two doubles, one run in and the tying run in scoring position. It was the most promising inning the Rockies had had against Hoffman since they rallied for four in the bottom of the ninth on Opening Day in 2005, when Clint Barmes ended the game with a two-run homer for a 12-10 victory. The unfolding scene triggered a memory in Ryan Speier.

"My mind went back to my very first game in the big leagues," he recalled, "when we walked-off Trevor Hoffman on Opening Day. I actually got the win in that game. I'm thinking, 'This guy doesn't like to pitch in this place. I'm sure of it. So, we'll see.'

"Being a closer," Speier continued, "I saw Trevor get up a few times. And I know how that can be, not only physically demanding but also mentally exhausting. It's kind of a letdown, not in that you're disappointed but in that you're up emotionally and then you're down. It wears you out emotionally. I've been there before."

Matt Holliday, whose misplay in the eighth gave the Padres life, was next. He was 0-for-2 against Hoffman so far in 2007, and Game 163 had so far shown both the good and the ugly of even a legitimate MVP candidate. In addition to his gaffe on the fly ball hit by Giles, he had singled to score Tulowitzki and tie the game 5-5 in the fifth, but had struck out against Peavy to end the sixth with Tulowitzki on third with the run that would have extended Colorado's lead to 7-5. This was his chance for redemption, a chance to cap a great season.

"This game goes much longer," Joe Simpson had observed after Holliday's strikeout his last time at bat in the 11th, *"that batting title will come into question again. Holliday's inching a little backward, down closer to Chipper Jones. He's a point-and-a-half ahead right now."*

Holliday wasted no time clinching that batting title—and winning the NL RBI crown—lining Hoffman's first pitch to deep right field. It banged high off the out-of-town scoreboard—which still displayed all of the final scores of Sunday's season-ending games for everyone else, including those losses by Boston and Atlanta that Orsillo and Simpson had called. The ball bounded back past Giles as he bounced off the scoreboard himself. Tulowitzki scored easily, and Holliday wound up at third with the Rockies' third triple of the game.

"When Matty hit the ball, I thought it was gone," said Jamey

Carroll, who was watching from the crowded Rockies dugout. In the third base coaching box, Gallego had the same feeling.

"I thought, 'Game over.' I thought it was out of the ballpark. I thought, 'We got this.' Then it hits off the wall, and he comes in with a triple.

"I'm like, 'Omigod.'"

"Giles did everything he could to make this catch," said Simpson. *"He just wasn't tall enough."*

"People don't know this," Josh Bard revealed in 2020. "Hoffy was pitching hurt. Most of the guys on the field at that point, Game 163, are playing hurt in some way. He'd been pitching for a month banged up; he was having some elbow issues. He's just such a competitor; he had pitched well. (But) it wasn't traditional Hoffy. I know he would never have put himself in a position to hurt the team. Everybody on the team wanted him out there because he's the ultimate competitor."

Unexpectedly, following Holliday's triple 'Gags' found himself in the same situation he'd been in with Seth Smith half-a-game-ago. Well, almost.

"This conversation was a little different. I still have bruises on my hands. Whenever he gave you a high-five after a big hit—this guy was as strong as an ox. All I remember is how hard he hit my hand. I'm not thinking about the score anymore. All I'm thinking about is, 'Is my hand broken?'

"He couldn't even talk. He was so pumped up. He was like a linebacker—at least, what I think a big linebacker must be like after he's made a big play. His eyes were so big. His breath was heavy. Now the crowd is loud. I'm trying to talk to him, and he can't hear me."

'Gags' calls coaching third base "the closest you can get to being still a player. Because you're running the bases with each and every one of these guys." He also believes, "The third base coach probably has more of an impact than the manager does." Managers may beg to differ, but Gallego makes a good argument in support of his opinion.

"It's definitely a job for somebody who has a good heart and doesn't have high blood pressure. It's a thankless job. You're nervous all day long.

"If you send somebody and he gets thrown out, everyone goes, 'Why'd you send him?' If you don't send somebody, and the outfielder bobbles the ball or it's a bad throw, they look at you and go, 'Why didn't you send him?' And when you do send him and he gets in there by a step, people go, 'What a great baserunning job that kid did.'

"But that's okay. Because you know you have a huge impact on every game."

The winning run was at third with no outs, and Todd Helton, who had the Rockies' only hit off Hoffman in the future Hall of Fame closer's five 2007 appearances against Colorado before Game 163, was next. A few weeks earlier, on September 8, Helton had swung and missed at a 74-mile-per-hour changeup to become Hoffman's one thousandth strikeout victim—1,000 strikeouts in only 917 innings! But Helton was 13-for-22 lifetime against Hoffman, and with Carroll, a righthanded batter with a .225 average on deck, an intentional walk made more sense than challenging a lifetime .300-plus hitter who already had a home run and two RBIs in the game.

"When you've got a choice of trying to pitch to Helton to avoid the season ending, or Jamey Carroll," Simpson had said when Helton walked and Carroll came next in the 11th, *"the odds are in your favor if you pitch to Carroll."*

Jamey Carroll was not someone who had his major league career handed to him, not by any means. Drafted in the 14th round of the 1996 amateur draft after a solid four seasons at the University of Evansville, he had toiled in the minor leagues for seven years before finally being a September callup of the Montreal Expos in 2002. His list of stops en route hints at the itinerancy that followed being drafted: Burlington, Vermont . . . West Palm Beach, Florida . . . Harrisburg, Pennsylvania (four times) . . . Ottawa, Canada (three times). He was 29 in his full rookie season (2003), when he batted .260 in 105 games. He improved to .289 the next season and etched his name into Expos history by scoring the team's final run before the franchise relocated to Washington for the 2005 season.

At 33, he was halfway through 12 years in the majors (six teams, seven cities) as he stepped in against Trevor Hoffman with Matt Holliday on third and Todd Helton on first. In two seasons with the Rockies, Carroll had hit better at Coors Field than anywhere in his career—.313 in 120 games and 427 plate appearances. Against San Diego in 2007, home and road combined, he was 5-for-27. He was the batter now only because Garret Atkins' seventh-inning drive had been ruled a double instead of a homer and Carroll had been sent in to run for him to improve Colorado's chances of scoring from second on an ensuing hit—which never came.

"We'd been playing this way the last month, especially with the 40-man roster," Carroll explained. "When we got up, I would go in for defense for Garrett. And if we were to go down or blow the lead, because it was the 40-man roster, Ian Stewart would come in and hit for me.

"I didn't have a good year at the plate, at all, in 2007. So, I'm on deck, and I'm fully believing I'm not going to hit. I'm standing on deck, and when they walked Todd, I'm fully waiting for Clint to call my name. Brad Hawpe walks out, because he was on deck, and he says to me, 'Go up there and win this game.'"

At least one person close to the team was not surprised that Hurdle let Carroll bat. "I didn't think Clint was going to pinch hit for Jamey," said O'Dowd, "because I knew he was looking for someone to put the ball in play. And Jamey didn't strike out."

That didn't occur to Carroll, though. "I walk to home plate, and the whole time I'm fully expecting Clint to yell my name for me to come back. I was fully assuming that I wasn't going to hit."

Hurdle, though, never considered hitting for Carroll.

"You can say, 'Hit for him.' But what are your options after that? He's a professional hitter. Why take him out to go with somebody with less experience. He's been in the flow of the game. He's got the sweat going. He's engaged. He's involved."

"When I got to the plate," Carroll said, "I was like, 'This is reality.'"

Play at the plate

Trevor Hoffman peered in for the pitch sign from his catcher, who instead of Josh Bard, the ex-Cherry Creek star who had started the game behind the plate, was Michael Barrett. He had entered the game as part of that double switch in the seventh inning when Heath Bell relieved Jake Peavy and had made the last out when the Padres threatened against Herges in the 12th.

Barrett had come to the Padres from the Cubs in mid-June, lugging plenty of baggage with him. Just weeks before the trade, he'd needed stitches in his lip after an in-game fracas with pitcher Carlos Zambrano—his battery mate that day. The season before he'd received a 10-game suspension after instigating a brawl between the Cubs and White Sox by punching opposing catcher A.J. Pierzynski. And before that, in 2004, Barrett had nearly come to blows with Houston ace Roy Oswalt twice in one week, resulting in both benches emptying onto the field each time. Just a month after joining the Padres, he received a one-game suspension for arguing with home plate umpire Chris Guccione over a called third strike in the fifth inning of a 9-0 loss to Philadelphia.

Nevertheless, he was a highly regarded catcher, with a .994 fielding average in three full seasons in Chicago (2004-2006), to go with a .289 batting average and 60 runs batted in per year.

As with Herges, Barrett had been Carroll's teammate with the Expos after Carroll's callup in September 2002 and during all of 2003. They'd played together in the Montreal farm system before that. But they didn't acknowledge each other in this moment the way Carroll and Blum had at second base back in the seventh.

"It's Game 163 and it's a tie ball game," Jamey said. "At that point in time, I was preparing for the situation. There was nothing to be said."

Barrett went out to talk with Hoffman, and Black quickly joined them. Gesturing to his outfielders, he moved them closer to the infield in hopes of preventing a single over the drawn-in infield, and having a play at the plate on a shallow fly. Orsillo and Simpson discussed whether Clint Hurdle might try a squeeze play even though he'd called for only two in his managerial career. Carroll had laid down a sacrifice bunt successfully 28 times in the past three seasons, including six in 2007, but Hurdle ruled that out after considering it.

Game 163

"I felt like that would be a forced move," Hurdle explained. "My thought was, 'I've tried to stay out of the way.' I wanted to give him the freedom of having the at-bat to drive the run in."

Choking up on the bat just slightly, Carroll took his stance as Hoffman again looked to his catcher for the sign indicating what the first pitch should be.

"I'm looking at this situation in front of me," Carroll recalled, "and for me, playing with Michael Barrett as long as I had, he knew that I wasn't a first-pitch swinger. I never did; I was very low-percentage in my career of doing that. Knowing that you've got Trevor Hoffman on the hill, who likes to start fastball away, and knowing his changeup was something you didn't want to be a part of, I was trying to put my game plan into play and saying that, if I was ever going to swing at a first pitch, this is when I'm going to do it, because he's going to be fastball away. So, I anticipated it, looked for it, and fortunately I got it and was able to get enough on it."

Carroll sliced Hoffman's first pitch toward Brian Giles in right field. Giles already had played a prominent role in the game, scoring on Gonzalez's grand slam in the third inning, driving in the tying run on Holliday's misplay in the eighth, scoring the go-ahead run on Hairston's homer in the 13th, and making a valiant effort to catch Holliday's triple off the scoreboard the previous batter. Now, he would be part of the deciding play.

Jamey Carroll's liner was a lot like his hit to right just after Simpson's comment in the eleventh inning. At third base, there was no question what 'Gags' intended to do.

"We had just tied the game against the best closer in the game," he said. "We're going to keep going with this. You don't get too many opportunities to have a closer like that on the ropes. You don't get too many chances to score. You have to push the envelope. You have to take a chance. With the way we were rolling, I was betting on the Rockies.

"Matty's first movement was toward home. I thought the ball was going to be down on the ground, or in the gap, or down the line. He did, too. So, his first movement was toward home. He came back to third, and I'm like, 'There's no way I'm going to try to stop this guy.'

"Can you imagine, if I had held this guy up? You can't think that way. I'm thinking aggressively; he's thinking aggressively. All I'm thinking is, 'Tag up.'

"I depended on my reports. Brian Giles closed better on ground balls. On fly balls, he had a tendency to come in a little high."

What followed has been debated since that moment.

"We talk about emotions going up and down so much in this game," Carroll mused. "When I first hit it, the emotions went, 'Yes!' Then, seeing Giles standing right there, you're like, 'Oh no; it may not be.' Then when I see the ball released from his hand, I think, 'Oh, it's high.' Then I turn around, and I watch Michael catch it and see where Holliday was. It's like time stopped. What took only a few seconds seemed like a minute in time."

Watching from the dugout, Herges saw Holliday break and Giles throw. He knew it would be a close play.

"I can't believe the throw Giles made," he said. "Giles made the throw of his life. You're talking about time standing still right there. Not one breath was taken in a three-second period."

Barrett placed his left foot where the third base line tracked to home plate as he fielded the throw from Giles on a bounce. Holliday dove headfirst, crashing on his chin as he slid past Barrett in a cloud of dust. The ball bounded away, and home plate umpire Tim McClelland—known for his slow, deliberate strike calls—eventually signaled Holliday safe.

Immediately, the Padres complained that the runner never touched home.

"I'm not sure he got the plate," Orsillo said.

"I don't know that he did, either," Simpson agreed. *"Barrett looked like he blocked him off the plate."*

As they watched a replay, Simpson wondered aloud why McClelland delayed making the call.

"Usually when that play occurs, the umpire makes an instant call, so everybody knows. But when he hesitated, that

gave Barrett a chance to go get the ball, thinking he had blocked him off the plate."

"Obviously, we made the right decision to go," 'Gags' declared years later, tongue-in-cheek. "His pinkie nicked that plate."

In the scene at home plate, Holliday was as unsteady as a boxer who had been floored by a knockout punch. "Even if he'd needed to go back and touch home plate, he couldn't have done it," Herges said. "He was dazed." And in the clubhouse later, "He's sitting there with this huge 'strawberry' on his chin," Herges continued, "and he's saying, 'I really don't remember what happened. I remember trying to score, and that was it.'"

That was it, alright. The Rockies had denied the disbelieving Padres.

Looking back on Game 163's finish, one of two heartbreaking defeats in a three-day span, Bud Black said, "It just goes to show you that it's so close, winning and losing. And championship games, it's razor-thin sometimes . . . That was a tough one for us, no doubt about it."

If it's true that "One man's trash is another man's treasure," as the old saying goes, the Game 163 adaptation in 2007 might go, "One man's crash is another man's pleasure."

Such was the case in the immediate aftermath of the Rockies unexpected 13th-inning rally against Trevor Hoffman. Colorado's bloated bench erupted with unrestrained glee, and the

Game 163

Coors Field crowd danced and whistled and high-fived into the night. In the shadows, meanwhile, the vanquished visitors were stunned, even more than heartbroken—no one more than Hoffman, who walked, head down, to the San Diego dugout then into the clubhouse, where a scene unfolded that Josh Bard calls "one of the neatest moments I've ever seen in baseball."

As Hoffman sat by his locker, the disappointment obvious, his teammates rallied around him.

"At the end of the day it was a unique experience, watching that in the locker room," Bard said. "It was one of the toughest locker rooms ever. Hoffy was just crushed. To see, literally, every guy on the team go over and just console him and tell him how much they appreciated him and how much they knew he gutted it out—as far as clubhouse moments, it was a pretty special thing, even though it was in a heartbreaking time.

"There's no better teammate," Bard said of Hoffman. "He was the heart and soul of our club. It's very rare that your best player is your hardest worker—the best guy, the guy that brings everybody together."

Trevor's mom had taught her son to take responsibility for what he did. "Bad workmen always blame their tools," Mikki Hoffman would say. And so, with the bitter taste of a crushing loss still fresh, Hoffman faced an inquisition in the locker room as sportswriters pressed him to explain what had just happened—and how.

"I can't," he said. "I'm having a hard time doing that. It's not like I don't want to express it. But to play in that game, and the way it was, the way everybody participated the way they did, and the way it turned out the way it did, it's hard to do.

"It happened pretty quick," he said. "Everything felt really good out there. I just couldn't get the job done."

When questioners posed possible explanations—Coors Field . . . repeatedly warming up . . . an extra game the day after the regular season was supposed to end—he eschewed excuses.

"There aren't many clichés you can give in this situation," he responded. "You cannot point to any other factor than my performance. That's a burden I'm going to have to deal with.

"I'm a professional, man," he also said. "It doesn't matter where you're at. You've got to be ready to go wherever you're at."

And, "I can't sit here and overanalyze things at this stage. People want to see execution and their ballclub move forward. That didn't happen tonight for one glaring reason—me."

The way San Diego's closer and team leader stood tall is something Warren Miller, Padres Media Relations Director at the time (and coincidentally, Rockies Director of Communications beginning in 2015) would always remember.

"My greatest memory of Trevor," Miller later said, "is from game number 163 in 2007. Seeing his passion for the Padres, his love for his teammates and his devastation over the loss, then watching him handling each reporter's question with the utmost class and professionalism ranks as my greatest sports memory. How he handled that incredible loss says more about him than any save could. Life is about how you handle adversity, and what he demonstrated that night was just remarkable."

On the field, Craig Sager cornered Jamey Carroll, repeating Simpson's line from earlier that "you never know who the hero will be." Then he asked about the final at-bat.

"I was just trying to put the ball in play," Carroll said, still overcome by it all. "I'm just thankful Matty ran his butt off to get to home plate . . . I know one thing," he added. "My mom's up in Heaven, and I guarantee you she was knocking on God's arm, telling him to make this happen for us."

What wasn't explained that day were the circumstances surrounding that comment by Carroll. Patty Carroll, 56, was hospitalized with pneumonia in early December 2005. Within a day she unexpectedly died of septic shock.

"A short time after that I was traded to Colorado," Jamey said. "I went into a situation, first time I'd ever played with a different team, and I was welcomed with open arms. I was fresh off trauma in my life, losing my mom. My mom's favorite color was purple, and I was traded to a team that is purple—the only team that is purple in the big leagues. In '06 I had the best year of my career. The next season, I had the worst year in my career, yet team-wise it was the best. I just felt like something bigger was playing at that time."

Sager wanted to ask more questions, but Carroll cut him off as politely as he could.

"I want to go celebrate, if you don't mind."

The 'Pine Tar Ump'

The 6-foot-6 home plate umpire who ruled Holliday safe at home with the run that sent the Rockies into the National League Division Series in Philadelphia was no stranger to big games or controversial calls (as Orsillo and Simpson alluded in the sixth inning). Among more than 4,200 games that Tim McClelland umpired between 1983 and 2013 were four World Series, nine League Championship Series, five Division Series and three All-Star Games. He was widely considered one of baseball's top umpires, once voted "best" by major league players in a *Sports Illustrated* poll.

In what must qualify as umpiring for the cycle, he was the home plate umpire for David Wells' perfect game against the Twins at Yankee Stadium in 1998; was at first base when Detroit's Jack Morris no-hit the White Sox in 1984; was the second base ump for Philip Humber's perfect game for the White Sox at Seattle in 2012; and worked third base during Nolan Ryan's sixth no-hitter at Oakland in 1990.

Among other noteworthy moments in a career that made him the second-longest-serving umpire in baseball history behind Joe West is the 2003 game at Wrigley Field when Cubs slugger Sammy Sosa was caught with a corked bat, which resulted in his ejection and a one-game suspension. "I turned it over and there was a small, probably half-dollar-size piece of cork in the bat right about halfway down the barrelhead, I guess," McClelland said after the game. "It was notched in there. I felt it and it obviously was cork, so I called the crew together, and it was reminiscent of what happened about 20 years ago with me."

"About 20 years ago" was when McClelland became known as "The Pine Tar Umpire" for disallowing a home run by Kansas City Hall of Famer and three-time batting champion George Brett during a game at Yankee Stadium. It was 1983, McClelland's debut season. The Yankees were leading 4-3 with U L Washington on first base and two outs. Hard-throwing closer Goose Gossage—one of Colorado Springs' favorite sons—had been called from the bullpen to face Brett.

"When Goose pitches against right-handers, he throws some sliders," Brett was quoted years later. "But I'm a lefty. Mostly, Goose is just, 'Hey, I'm going to throw it as hard as I can. If you hit it, congratulations—I hope you hit it at somebody. If you don't, good job.' He was a power guy, not a finesse guy."

Brett hit Goose's first pitch home run distance but foul. Then he fouled the next pitch outside first. The 0-2 pitch was up and in, but Brett tomahawked it into the right field seats for a two-run homer and a 5-4 Royals lead.

As Brett rounded the bases, Yankees manager Billy Martin grabbed the bat from the Kansas City batboy and handed it to McClelland. (Martin had spotted an issue with Brett's bat before the game began but strategically waited to raise an issue until it mattered.) As Brett crossed home plate, Martin was talking to McClelland, who was holding Brett's bat. The discussion went on and on until McClelland laid Brett's bat across home plate. The plate is seventeen inches wide, and the baseball rulebook states the maximum allowable length of pine tar on a bat from the knob is eighteen inches; the pine tar obviously exceeded the length limit. Seconds later McClelland approached the Royals dugout, looking for Brett. When he found him, he said, "You're out." (That, cracked one writer, made Brett the only player in history to hit a game-losing home run.)

Brett erupted from the dugout, livid. He pointed his finger at McClelland and screamed. Kansas City's manager, the late Dick Howser, got between Brett and McClelland, and umpire Joe Brinkman and a couple of Brett's teammates tried to restrain Brett from behind. One of those teammates was Joe Simpson, the same Joe Simpson who had just witnessed McClelland call Matt Holliday safe at home from the TBS booth.

"I had to get crew chief Joe Brinkman off of George," Simpson recalled, "because Joe was afraid to let him go."

American League President Lee MacPhail later overruled McClelland, explaining that any equipment-related objection must be made prior to the play. Brett's home run counted; three weeks later the game was resumed with two outs in the top of the ninth; and the Royals won 5-4 after closer Dan Quisenberry retired New York in order in the bottom of the ninth for his 33rd save. (Kansas City's starting pitcher that day was San Diego's manager 24 years later in Game 163—Bud Black. He allowed all four Yankee runs and seven hits in six innings.)

In Game 163 McClelland called balls and strikes for a whopping 129 batters (169 balls and 257 strikes, for a total of 426 pitches). That's almost double a normal, nine-inning game, but it wasn't his personal record. Five years after the "pine tar game," on Sunday, September 12, 1988—also at Yankee Stadium—he was behind the plate for all 564 pitches of the New York-Detroit 18-inning marathon that saw 139 batters go to bat in six hours and one minute. (The Yankees won, 5-4, on a two-run, walk-off homer by Claudell Washington after Sparky Anderson's Tigers had taken the lead on an error, a sacrifice bunt and Torey Lovullo's single in the top of the inning.)

"That's a lot of squatting (behind the catcher)," McClelland once said of the prolonged Game 163. A few batters questioned a few calls, but for such a tense game, McClelland's performance drew compliments. During one TBS studio break, Iron Man Cal Ripken, the player who broke Lou Gehrig's seemingly unbreakable record for consecutive games played with 2,632, told host Ernie Johnson, "I'm watching this game and I'm agreeing with everything he's calling. He's doing a really nice job on the plate tonight."

"You're not still playing," Johnson chided. "You don't really need to say, 'I haven't disagreed with a single thing he's done; he's doing a great job.'"

"I'll tell you when I think he's calling a bad game," Ripken replied with a smile, taking up the banter. "He's calling a great game."

Balls and strikes aside, McClelland's final call of the game—SAFE!—will forever be debated by Padres fans. Even many Rockies wonder if Holliday was safe. There was no basis, however, for reconsideration by Major League Baseball. It was a judgment call, just like Tschida's decision on the ball hit by Atkins. Looking back at both cases, existing replays were, at best, inconclusive.

Joe Simpson, though, saw it differently, even 13 years later. Reflecting his experience as a player, he said:

"I have great respect for McClelland, excellent umpire and a long career. However, he messed up that call in the 13th.

"Every player knows that on a close tag play at the plate, the umpire will signal safe or out. The catcher also knows that if NO signal is given, then the runner missed the plate and the play is still live. The umpire is essentially telling the catcher 'you need to tag him!'

"Michael Barrett looked at Tim and got NO signal, so he scrambled to go back and tag Matt Holliday. In those seconds leading up to that tag, suddenly, McClelland threw up a safe sign. It was horribly delayed and, per the replay, incorrect.

"That's what upset Barrett so much, and rightfully so. Why was there a 'no call' and suddenly a safe call? Watch the replay. Watch Barrett looking at Tim, then hustle to go back to Holliday to tag him (again). Barrett got mixed signals (no call) and then yelled at McClelland for good reason."

McClelland missed the 2014 season with a back injury and retired in early 2015. "I'm putting baseball behind me," he told the *Des Moines Register* then, and since has declined all interview requests. He has said that he stopped paying attention to baseball to enjoy retirement with his wife and family. Asked about Game 163's length, he once said that he didn't feel tired until he was back in the umpire's room afterwards. He at first didn't realize the game was in extra innings, he said, and as it wore on, he focused only on his job and trying to get every call right.

Thirteen years later Josh Bard still had not watched a video of Game 163, and probably never would. But he knew what he believed about the fateful call and was philosophical about the outcome.

"Do I think he touched home plate? No. But we can't do anything about that. If you don't like it, you gotta play better. We put ourselves in that situation.

"It's an all-time game in the history of major league baseball—two teams competing—and we came out on the short end of the stick. It's frustrating, but you move forward."

Jamey Carroll's conclusion, as one would expect, is a bit different.

"I've watched it a million times," he said. "I gotta believe somewhere in there, yes, with so much dirt kicking up, Matty got his hand in there." And then he adds, "The umpire thought so, so I think so, as well."

Matt Herges also watched the TBS telecast several times in the years that followed, and his take is similar to Carroll's.

"Back then," he said, "the cameras and the angles weren't as good as they are now. I don't think there's an umpire alive who wouldn't have called him safe. No human eye can see when he was jamming his hand into Michael's foot. There's a slight possibility that maybe a fingertip touched the plate."

Dan O'Dowd was another who went with Tim McClelland's decision and agreed with Herges.

"I think if you'd had replay," he said, "it would have been inconclusive. I'm going to say he touched home plate because

I'd be an idiot not to say that. I don't think any of us know."

Don Orsillo, though, demurs. Asked what moments in Game 163 stand out in his memory, he answered:

"For me it's the one play that mattered. Matt Holliday's headfirst slide to the plate. I said at the time I am not sure he ever got there, and I am still not sure 13 years later that he ever did.

"Personally, after four hours and 40 minutes of my first national game, I just wanted to make the call correctly and not be wrong. I made the call, but I am mostly sure the umpires did not."

'Holliday Touched It'

The Rockies had fun with the momentous 13th inning decision in a TV commercial titled "Holliday Touched It" that aired the next season. Posted to YouTube and viewed by thousands (as of 2020), the 30-second spoof spot went like this:

> Clint Hurdle is sitting at a table in the Rockies clubhouse, reading the newspaper. A jelly donut sits on a plate, on the otherwise empty table. Matt Holliday walks by and Hurdle calls to him.
>
> "Holliday! Did you touch that?"
>
> The camera zeroes in on the donut on the plate, and Brad Hawpe jumps up front his locker and walks toward the table.

"I think he touched it," Hawpe says, pointing at the donut.

"Oh, yeah," Hurdle says. "You touched it. We all saw it. Didn't we, men."

By now, three other teammates—Clint Barmes, Jeff Francis and Garrett Atkins—have joined Hawpe around the table. The accused is facing them all. Talking over each other, they all agree that he touched it.

"Did you?" Hurdle asks again. "Did you touch that?"

"Yeah, I touched it," Holliday finally answers. Then he picks up the donut and takes a bite out of it.

As he walks away, jelly is on his chin—right where the "strawberry" was after his dive to the plate in the 13th inning of Game 163.

(The spot wraps up with audio of Jeff Kingery's radio call of the play at the plate and what is known in advertising as a billboard, in this case, ticket sales information.)

The commercial was part of a campaign that won a national sports marketing award in 2008. Written in-house by a team that included Jill Campbell (who became Rockies vice president – Communications & Marketing in 2016), Brady O'Neil and

Camden Kelley, it was the product of an elaborate brainstorming process within the Rockies organization.

"Everything we did from a scripting standpoint was a collaboration," Campbell said in 2020. "The majority of scripts each year came from within our Rockies' creative group (about 10 individuals from various departments in the organization).

"Each Rockies brainstorm meeting would consist of reading through each script aloud, gauging reaction from the group and fine-tuning, ultimately coming to an agreement on the best elements to work into the final script—including which players would work best for each role, based on internal knowledge of our Rockies players, in terms of their personalities and what we felt like certain players would feel comfortable saying on a commercial set.

"After several Rockies brainstorm sessions, we would select our favorite 10-15 scripts to pitch to Rockies officers. For this part, I would meet with each officer individually, reading each script aloud (and gauging their reactions, as another "test market"). The officers would select their six favorites."

Eventually a consensus was reached on which six scripts would be produced. Blue Goose Productions of Seattle filmed "Holliday Touched It"—as well as other humorous Rockies commercials at this time.

"We'd shot comedy commercials for the Seattle Mariners (since 1995)," said Ron Gross, who suggested making the donut-based skit, submitted a first draft script which the Rockies trio polished, then directed the shoot. "That's how I met Kent Krosbakken, who worked in the front office of the Rockies. He had been with the Mariners organization, and when he went to the Rockies (in 2005), he called us and said, 'Hey, I think we'd like to start doing that.'"

Gross frequently contributed ideas and often submitted first-draft scripts that went through the brainstorming process. If adopted, they were then tweaked, as was the case with Holliday. He directed Rockies comedy commercials for seven years, and his impressions from January 2008 jibed with everything others said about the Game 163 victors.

"There was an interesting different culture from the Mariners at the Rockies," Gross said. "It had everything to do with, I think, the DNA of that ballclub. These ballplayers had all come up through the minor leagues together, and that made a very different feeling in the clubhouse. In interacting with the organization and the marketing team, it was my understanding that Keli McGregor really set the tone. I'm sure Keli was one of the important voices in saying, 'We're going to do these as ensemble pieces. Nobody gets their own spot; that's not our culture here. Everybody laughs together.'

"When we wrote commercials for the Mariners, we were always writing a Griffey commercial, or a Randy Johnson commercial, or a Jay Buhner commercial, or an Edgar Martinez commercial, or an Ichiro Suzuki commercial, or an Alex Rodriguez commercial. All of those commercials were tailored for one of the stars. In the Rockies clubhouse, when we started working for them, we started that approach, and they said, 'No, no, no, no, no. That's not us. We want all the spots we do to be ensemble spots. We don't want a commercial focused on just one of our players. We want to do this comedy, but we want them to be ensemble pieces.' I always thought that was an interesting difference."

The "Holliday Touched It" commercial was shot in the Rockies clubhouse at Coors Field.

"The ballclub would always bring their players to Denver around the end of January, early February," Gross said, "to get all of their eye exams, their physicals and all that stuff out of the way before spring training started. We'd bring in a crew of 12 to 15, which is actually small for a film crew, and routinely did as many as six or seven commercials in two or sometimes three days. These things were almost like an expedition to organize. My partner, executive producer Bill Hoare, was a master at organizing them to get them all done in a couple days.

"Most filmmaking," Gross continued, "we're in charge. We get to play offense. But when you're working with those athletes and those organizations, you're not the most important thing. They have a lot to do, even in January. So, we're on defense; we have to shoot these things in a very disciplined manner. What would generally take eight hours, we'd get done in an hour or two—with non-professional talent, these players."

Gross conceded that "non-professional" doesn't exactly describe major league ballplayers serving as acting talent.

"Talk about performance anxiety," Gross mused dismissively. "These guys are performers of the highest order. What I was asking them to do in front of a camera, in my mind, paled in comparison to even fielding a ground ball at second base on a major league baseball diamond."

Gross credited Rockies manager Clint Hurdle, whose astute direction in the dugout led the Rockies to the World Series, with making "Holliday Touched It" such a natural skit.

"It was all scripted," Gross said.

"But," he added, reciting one of the adages of his business, "just because it's good on the page doesn't mean it's gonna be good on the stage—unless they make it that way."

Recalling the scene where Hurdle is seated at the table in the locker room and Hawpe, Francis, Atkins and Barmes gather behind him to confront Holliday as a group, Gross added: "This is where a person like Clint, as kind of the ringleader, makes the difference. It was natural for him, and for the players—because he was their leader."

More than a decade later, Gross continued to appreciate the former Rockies manager.

"Clint Hurdle became one of my favorites to work with," he said. "Nice man. And just really good in front of the camera.

Of all the people I've worked with doing comedy commercials, he is certainly in my top five of people who just get it and is a really wonderful comedic actor."

The jelly-induced "strawberry" on Holliday's chin after he grabs the donut from the table and bites into it was painted on his chin, Gross revealed.

"When we mentioned it, Holliday got a big kick out of it. He nodded, laughed and said, 'That's good.'

"Honestly," Gross said, "if you knew that play and studied it, recreating the 'strawberry' from that head-first slide was a pretty obvious, fun thing to do."

Three more sweeps

Just as the question "Did Holliday touch home plate?" will live on in baseball lore, so, too, will some variation of, "Did the Rockies win their way to the World Series too quickly?"

Colorado, which won the season series against the Phillies 4-3, beat Philadelphia three straight in the Division Series. Holliday hit two home runs; Torrealba hit .500 (5-for-10) and Matsui .417 with a grand slam; and Manny Corpas saved all three games. But while the red-hot Rockies also swept Arizona in four—ending with Todd Helton raising both arms in triumph and relief as Garrett Atkins' throw beat Eric Byrnes' head-first slide for the last out—it took the Boston Red Sox seven games to dispose of Cleveland after sweeping the Angels. Rallying from a 3-1 deficit, Boston won the last three games by lopsided scores of 7-1, 12-2 and 11-2.

That meant more than a week passed between Colorado's pennant-clinching celebration in the Coors Field infield on October 15 and the first game of the World Series in Boston on October 24. Cooled off while the Red Sox were just a couple days from the last of three dominating victories in a row, the Rockies lost four straight, leading only once—for the first three innings of Game Two.

Was it Boston's pitching, which allowed only 10 runs in four games, including only one each in the first two?

Was the Boston offense, which reached double figures twice while scoring 29, just that much better?

Were the Red Sox the hot team, rather than the Rockies, by the time the Series began?

Would the outcome have been any different if the Rockies had been able to just keep on playing after winning four in a row from the Diamondbacks, instead of sitting around for nine days?

Mike Gallego had been in a similar situation once before, the 10-day delay between Game Two and Game Three of The Earthquake Series.

"Tony literally brought us back to our spring training site during that time," he recalled, "and he had us play intrasquad games. And he told us these intrasquad games weren't going to be typical intrasquad games. We were going to play with intensity. We were going to try to

GAME 163

break up the double plays; we were going to brush people back. Against each other!

"He knew this layoff could deflate any hot team. It was Tony LaRussa who decided it was going to be a different mindset for the time off, and we all bought into it."

(When the series resumed, Oakland won Games Three and Four to complete a sweep of the Giants.)

That is not to say, however, that Gallego feels Clint Hurdle erred in the way he handled the layoff while the Rockies waited for the winner of the Boston-Cleveland series.

"We were coming to the ballpark, taking batting practice, taking a few ground balls, and going to dinner. Maybe because we were young and maybe because it was the first time for everybody, maybe it was time to relax a little after what we just went through, those 21 games. Nothing more intense than all those series: We had to beat the Dodgers, the Phillies—and we had to wait for Milwaukee to beat the Padres.

"Are you kidding? The whole scenario was overwhelming and completely draining. We deserved some time off to just chill and relax."

Still, Gallego says: "I would have loved to have seen that team play a few days after (clinching the National League pennant)."

Dan O'Dowd agreed.

"The game of baseball, at that level at that time of year, is meant to be played every day," he said. "It's a game of balance, rhythm and timing. And it's like we took a collective breath after that emotional run for so long, and we lost our balance, rhythm and timing. Simple as that. And we could not get it back.

"The Red Sox were a great team," O'Dowd was quick to say, "and I don't know how it would have played out. But I do think, in my heart, it would have been an incredibly captivating series if we had been able to play right away. It was just too long of a layoff. That killed us. I'm sad, because I thought we had a chance to win a World Series. I feel bad that we were denied that opportunity, based on the quirk of schedule."

Hurdle looks at it much the same way.

"We got to play the best team in baseball, and they were hot," he says. "And they got to roll right into the Series.

"There's no doubt in my mind the layoff affected us. You can't recreate adrenaline. We had adrenaline. We had momentum. We had traction. We did everything we could to try to keep sharp over eight days of layoff. We weren't able to recreate that intensity.

"It affected us; however, that's not an excuse. It's what it was. It wasn't meant to happen. They beat us on the mound. They beat us at the plate. They beat us in the field."

Regardless, Rocktober 2007 was a time for the ages, highlighted by Game 163.

Author's Note

*"One of the beautiful things
about baseball is the history."*

JAMES ANTHONY ABBOTT

The quote from Bill Klem at the beginning of this book, and the quote above from Jim Abbott are the best I could find to capture the classic nature of the 2007 season's Game 163 between the Rockies and Padres. And the speakers are representative in themselves.

Bill Klem was a major league umpire (National League) across five decades, from 1905 to 1941, and is known as "the father of baseball umpires." He worked a record 18 World Series, and is in the Baseball Hall of Fame, inducted posthumously in 1953.

Holder of the major-league record for ejections by an umpire with 251, he once said of the pressure of umpiring: "Most baseball fans . . . feel that these verbal and physical public humiliations [umpires endure] go in one ear and out the other. Well, they don't. They go in one ear and go straight to the nervous system, eating away coordination, self-confidence and self-respect." Perhaps this explains why Tim McClelland, when he retired, told the *Des Moines Register*, "I'm putting baseball behind me."

Born without his right hand and a stub of forearm just below his elbow, Jim Abbott nonetheless became a part of baseball history, just like 2007's Game 163.

Tucking his glove in his armpit as he threw, then quickly putting his left hand in the glove to be ready to field his position, Abbott pitched for four teams in a 10-year career—the Angels, Yankees, White Sox and Brewers—and won 87 games. (He also lost 112.) He was an 18-game winner for the Angels in 1991 and threw a no-hitter for the Yankees in 1993. (He also lost 18 one year with California.) His earned run average was as low as 2.89, when he won 18, and 2.77 the next year, when he went 7-15. Yet the year he lost 18, it was 7.48.

In short, his decade in the major leagues had as many highs and lows as the 13-inning marathon between Colorado and San Diego on October 1, 2007.

Writing about a baseball game more than a decade after it was played has its advantages and its disadvantages.

The advantages are that everyone who was involved (and

— GAME 163 —

will talk about the game) is far enough removed from the moment that they speak freely and openly. And in most cases, they have vivid recollections—particularly if the game was memorable, as with Game 163 between the Rockies and Padres.

The disadvantages are finding those people, and reaching them to gather their memories, after they've moved into private life, or at least are no longer associated with the Rockies or Padres. (Not all who were contacted responded, and some who did declined to be interviewed.)

My thanks, then, go out to all who helped me track down the key figures I interviewed for this book, as well as those who tried but were unsuccessful. This includes: Dan Hart of the Pirates, Adam Chodzko of the Angels, Casey Wilcox of the Diamondbacks, Joe Jareck of the Dodgers, San Diego's Craig Hughner and J.P. Nolan, Oakland's Fernando Alcala, Warren Miller, who moved from the Padres to the Rockies in 2015, Lynn Worthy, Vahe Gregorian, Rusty Hampton, Rick Cleveland, Jason Mackey and our daughter, Melissa Sailer.

I owe a special Thank You to Mike Gallego, who not only shared great stories about being the Rockies' third base coach that night, but also recommended I interview Bill Geivett then lined it up for me. And to Clint Hurdle, who found ways to respond, even if it meant leaving answers on Voice Mail! Many have said Clint's the best, and I concur.

Others provided invaluable assistance, such as:

- Naomi Morishita of the University of Denver's Morgridge School of Education, who calculated the statistical probabilities cited in the One More Game chapter;

- Katie Steiner, who facilitated my licensing agreement with Major League Baseball regarding use of the telecast of the tiebreaker game in recreating the inning-by-inning account;

- Sean Forman, President of Sports Reference LLC, for permission to reprint the box score, play-by-play and other records from Baseball-Reference.com. The site was an invaluable source for this book, and the family of sports-reference sites is a not-to-miss online resource for every sports fan.

- Brian Trembath, Special Collections Librarian in the Western History & Genealogy Department at the Denver Public Library, for his help despite the Coronavirus lockdown in researching newspaper coverage of Game 163 and locating the image used on the cover; and

- Byron Hanson, who grew up a Cubs fans in the Ernie

Banks era and has the memorabilia to prove it, who provided invaluable feedback, assistance and guidance in the early stages of this project.

If this book reads well and looks great, the credit goes to my extraordinary editor, Jon Rizzi, and the most talented designer I know, Scott Johnson, whose talent is reflected in both the cover and throughout.

Above all, I thank my wife Melanie, who has shared my love of baseball for more than half a century, and who has supported my writing career for just as long. *Game 163* is just the most recent example of both.

As for the many who graciously and generously revisited the game, their revealing words within this book speak for themselves. (And, as often is the case, the best stories come from unlikely sources.) Those words, though, don't capture the friendliness and enthusiasm they all communicated as they answered question after question. Nor do they, in all cases, include personal stories that made writing this book even more fun.

One of my favorites came from pitcher Matt Herges, whose resolve carried the Rockies from the 10th to the 13th inning. He's relating a time when he was watching a replay of Game 163 with his son. He's trying to pass on some wisdom about pitching as they watch his first inning of work. It's classic "Do-as-I-say-not-as-I-do."

"I'm sitting there with my son, who pitches now in high school. And I tell him: 'Two outs, 2-0 counts; they kill you. Two-out walks are absolutely never something you can do.' I'm going over all this stuff, and he's sitting there, watching the replay, and he says, 'Holy cow. You just got two quick outs, and you've got a 2-0 count on Sledge.'"

Another, revealing the personal side of Rockies ace Jeff Francis, came from Ron Gross, who got to know many Rockies players while directing what he called the club's comedy commercials for seven seasons.

"Jeff Francis was fantastic. The big Canadian was very interested in filmmaking. He would actually show up and watch us shoot other commercials, which is really rare, just because he was interested in the process."

I asked each person I interviewed if Game 163 was the highlight of his career in baseball. A couple of responses that did not fit into the narrative are worth sharing here for the broader perspective they provide.

Jamey Carroll, whose liner drove in the winning run, said:

"For me, it's hard to say. I was fortunate to get to play in a spring training game with my younger brother Wes (against the Cardinals in Jupiter, Florida). First time that we ever played a game together. He's five years younger, so we always missed each other in high school and college. We got to turn a double play together.

"I was playing short and he was playing second. We were losing 8-0. It was a bases-loaded double play ball that, in the world, was meaningless. But to me, it was everything."

And Clint Hurdle, who managed the Pittsburgh Pirates for nine years after leading the Rockies from early 2002 to mid-2009, said:

"Two games are etched in my heart, that being one of them. The other was the blackout game we had in Pittsburgh in 2013. We snapped a 20-year losing streak—first time we had a winning season in 21 years. It was sold out; everyone showed up in black. That was a very significantly impactful game."

Sportscaster Don Orsillo added still another dimension:

"My first Red Sox game was the Hideo Nomo no-hitter at Camden Yards vs. the Orioles, April 4, 2001. My first game. A no-hitter. Tough to beat that."

One other realization is worth noting. I found truly remarkable the many connections between opponents in Game 163 who were former teammates, as well as the times during the final days of the 2007 season when two people with shared pasts crossed paths. What a small world professional baseball is!

And can there be any greater irony than Padres manager Bud Black, who 10 years later managed the Rockies to the Wild Card—in his first season in Colorado!

In a Game 163 10th anniversary story, Black admitted to "mixed emotions" then said: "The older I get, the more I appreciate that game, as far as being a great game. I don't think it gets the credit it deserves, partially because of the two teams, a little bit under-the-market-type teams. What a great game."

Appendix
Game 163 Batter-by-Batter and Boxscore

Score	Out	Batter	Pitcher	Count	Play Description
Top of the 1st, Padres Batting, Tied 0-0, Rockies' Josh Fogg facing 1-2-3					
0-0	0	Brian Giles	Josh Fogg	2-2	Groundout: 2B-1B (SS-2B)
0-0	1	Scott Hairston	Josh Fogg	2-2	Strikeout Swinging
0-0	2	Kevin Kouzmanoff	Josh Fogg	0-2	Single to RF (Fly Ball to Short RF)
0-0	2	Adrian Gonzalez	Josh Fogg	3-2	Strikeout Swinging
Bottom of the 1st, Rockies Batting, Tied 0-0, Padres' Jake Peavy facing 1-2-3					
0-0	0	Troy Tulowitzki	Jake Peavy	1-2	Single to SS (Ground Ball to Weak SS-2B); Matsui to 3B
0-0	0	Matt Holliday	Jake Peavy	3-1	Walk; Tulowitzki to 2B
0-0	0	Todd Helton	Jake Peavy	0-1	Flyball: CF/Sacrifice Fly (Deep CF); Matsui Scores; Tulowitzki to 3B; Holliday to 2B
1-0	1	Garrett Atkins	Jake Peavy	1-2	Single to LF (Line Drive to Short LF-CF); Tulowitzki Scores; Holliday to 3B
2-0	1	Brad Hawpe	Jake Peavy	1-2	Foul Popfly: 3B (3B into Foul Terr.)
2-0	2	Ryan Spilborghs	Jake Peavy	0-0	Flyball: CF (Deep CF-RF)
Top of the 2nd, Padres Batting, Behind 0-2, Rockies' Josh Fogg facing 5-6-7					
0-2	0	Khalil Greene	Josh Fogg	2-2	Strikeout Swinging
0-2	1	Josh Bard	Josh Fogg	2-2	Single to LF (Line Drive)
0-2	1	Geoff Blum	Josh Fogg	1-0	Flyball: RF (Deep CF-RF)
0-2	2	Brady Clark	Josh Fogg	1-0	Groundout: 3B-1B (Weak 3B)
Bottom of the 2nd, Rockies Batting, Ahead 2-0, Padres' Jake Peavy facing 8-9-1					
2-0	0	Yorvit Torrealba	Jake Peavy	2-1	Home Run (Fly Ball to Deep LF)
3-0	0	Josh Fogg	Jake Peavy	0-2	Strikeout Looking
3-0	1	Kazuo Matsui	Jake Peavy	1-0	Groundout: 2B-1B
3-0	2	Troy Tulowitzki	Jake Peavy	2-2	Strikeout Looking

Top of the 3rd, Padres Batting, Behind 0-3, Rockies' Josh Fogg facing 9-1-2

0-3	0	Jake Peavy	Josh Fogg	0-2	Single to CF (Ground Ball thru SS-2B)
0-3	0	Brian Giles	Josh Fogg	3-2	Walk; Peavy to 2B
0-3	0	Scott Hairston	Josh Fogg	0-1	Single to RF (Fly Ball to CF-RF); Peavy to 3B; Giles to 2B
0-3	0	Kevin Kouzmanoff	Josh Fogg	1-0	Flyball: LF (LF-CF)
0-3	1	Adrian Gonzalez	Josh Fogg	0-0	Home Run (Fly Ball to Deep RF); Peavy Scores; Giles Scores; Hairston Scores
4-3	1	Khalil Greene	Josh Fogg	0-0	Single to LF (Line Drive)
4-3	1	Josh Bard	Josh Fogg	0-0	Double to LF (Line Drive to LF Line); Greene to 3B
4-3	1	Geoff Blum	Josh Fogg	3-0	Intentional Walk
4-3	1	Brady Clark	Josh Fogg	0-0	Groundout: SS-2B/Forceout at 2B (Weak SS); Greene Scores; Bard to 3B
5-3	2	Jake Peavy	Josh Fogg	1-2	Lineout: 2B (SS-2B)

Bottom of the 3rd, Rockies Batting, Behind 3-5, Padres' Jake Peavy facing 3-4-5

3-5	0	Matt Holliday	Jake Peavy	2-2	Groundout: 2B-1B (SS-2B)
3-5	1	Todd Helton	Jake Peavy	0-0	Home Run (Fly Ball to Deep CF-RF)
4-5	1	Garrett Atkins	Jake Peavy	3-1	Walk
4-5	1	Brad Hawpe	Jake Peavy	2-2	Strikeout Swinging
4-5	2	Ryan Spilborghs	Jake Peavy	0-1	Groundout: 3B-2B/Forceout at 2B (Weak 3B)

Top of the 4th, Padres Batting, Ahead 5-4, Rockies' Josh Fogg facing 1-2-3

5-4	0	Brian Giles	Josh Fogg	0-0	Groundout: 2B-1B
5-4	1	Scott Hairston	Josh Fogg	1-2	Strikeout Looking
5-4	2	Kevin Kouzmanoff	Josh Fogg	2-2	Strikeout Looking

Bottom of the 4th, Rockies Batting, Behind 4-5, Padres' Jake Peavy facing 8-9-1

4-5	0	Yorvit Torrealba	Jake Peavy	0-0	Flyball: RF (Deep CF-RF)
4-5	1	Josh Fogg	Jake Peavy	2-1	Groundout: 2B-1B
4-5	2	Kazuo Matsui	Jake Peavy	3-1	Groundout: SS-1B (Weak SS)

Top of the 5th, Padres Batting, Ahead 5-4, Rockies' Josh Fogg facing 4-5-6

5-4	0	Adrian Gonzalez	Josh Fogg	0-0	Double to RF (Fly Ball to Deep CF-RF)

Taylor Buchholz replaces Josh Fogg pitching and batting 9th

5-4	0	Khalil Greene	Taylor Buchholz	1-1	Popfly: 2B (Short CF-RF)
5-4	1	Josh Bard	Taylor Buchholz	0-1	Lineout: LF (Deep LF-CF)
5-4	2	Geoff Blum	Taylor Buchholz	0-2	Strikeout Swinging

Bottom of the 5th, Rockies Batting, Behind 4-5, Padres' Jake Peavy facing 2-3-4

4-5	0	Troy Tulowitzki	Jake Peavy	3-2	Double to CF (Fly Ball to Deep LF-CF)
4-5	0	Matt Holliday	Jake Peavy	1-0	Single to CF (Line Drive to Short CF); Tulowitzki Scores
5-5	0	Todd Helton	Jake Peavy	0-0	Groundout: 3B-1B (Weak 3B); Holliday to 2B
5-5	1	Garrett Atkins	Jake Peavy	2-2	Strikeout Looking

— Game 163 —

5-5	2	Brad Hawpe	Jake Peavy	3-0	Intentional Walk
5-5	2	Ryan Spilborghs	Jake Peavy	2-2	Strikeout Swinging

Top of the 6th, Padres Batting, Tied 5-5, Rockies' Taylor Buchholz facing 8-9-1
5-5	0	Brady Clark	Taylor Buchholz	0-1	Single to CF (Ground Ball thru SS-2B)
5-5	0	Jake Peavy	Taylor Buchholz	0-2	Foul Bunt Popfly: C (Behind Home)

Jeremy Affeldt replaces Taylor Buchholz pitching and batting 9th
5-5	1	Brian Giles	Jeremy Affeldt	1-2	Wild Pitch; Clark to 2B
5-5	1	Brian Giles	Jeremy Affeldt	3-2	Popfly: SS (Weak SS-2B)

Ryan Speier replaces Jeremy Affeldt pitching and batting 9th
5-5	2	Scott Hairston	Ryan Speier	3-2	Strikeout Swinging

Bottom of the 6th, Rockies Batting, Tied 5-5, Padres' Jake Peavy facing 8-9-1
5-5	0	Yorvit Torrealba	Jake Peavy	1-0	Groundout: 3B-1B (Weak 3B)

Seth Smith pinch hits for Ryan Speier (P) batting 9th
5-5	1	Seth Smith	Jake Peavy	3-1	Triple to RF (Fly Ball to Deep CF)
5-5	1	Kazuo Matsui	Jake Peavy	1-2	Flyball: CF/Sacrifice Fly; Smith Scores
6-5	2	Troy Tulowitzki	Jake Peavy	0-1	Triple to LF (Fly Ball to Deep CF)
6-5	2	Matt Holliday	Jake Peavy	1-2	Strikeout Swinging

Top of the 7th, Padres Batting, Behind 5-6, Rockies' LaTroy Hawkins facing 3-4-5
LaTroy Hawkins replaces Seth Smith (PH) pitching and batting 9th
5-6	0	Kevin Kouzmanoff	LaTroy Hawkins	2-0	Groundout: 2B-1B (SS-2B)
5-6	1	Adrian Gonzalez	LaTroy Hawkins	3-2	Single to SS (Ground Ball to Weak SS)
5-6	1	Khalil Greene	LaTroy Hawkins	1-2	Strikeout Looking
5-6	2	Josh Bard	LaTroy Hawkins	0-1	Groundout: 2B-SS/Forceout at 2B

Bottom of the 7th, Rockies Batting, Ahead 6-5, Padres' Jake Peavy facing 4-5-6
6-5	0	Todd Helton	Jake Peavy	1-2	Lineout: 1B (2B-1B)
6-5	1	Garrett Atkins	Jake Peavy	0-0	Double to LF (Line Drive to Deep LF-CF)

Jamey Carroll pinch runs for Garrett Atkins (3B) batting 5th
6-5	1	Brad Hawpe	Jake Peavy	3-0	Intentional Walk

Heath Bell replaces Josh Bard (C) pitching and batting 6th
Michael Barrett replaces Jake Peavy (P) playing C batting 9th
6-5	1	Ryan Spilborghs	Heath Bell	1-2	Strikeout Swinging
6-5	2	Yorvit Torrealba	Heath Bell	3-2	Strikeout Swinging

Top of the 8th, Padres Batting, Behind 5-6, Rockies' Brian Fuentes facing 7-8-9
Brian Fuentes replaces Ryan Spilborghs (CF) pitching and batting 7th
Jamey Carroll moves from PR to 3B
Cory Sullivan replaces LaTroy Hawkins (P) playing CF batting 9th
5-6	0	Geoff Blum	Brian Fuentes	0-0	Single to CF (Line Drive)
5-6	0	Brady Clark	Brian Fuentes	0-1	Foul Popfly: 1B (1B into Foul Terr.)
5-6	1	Michael Barrett	Brian Fuentes	1-2	Strikeout Swinging, Wild Pitch; Blum to 2B
5-6	2	Brian Giles	Brian Fuentes	1-1	Double to LF (Fly Ball to Deep LF); Blum Scores
6-6	2	Scott Hairston	Brian Fuentes	0-1	Groundout: SS-1B (Weak SS)

Bottom of the 8th, Rockies Batting, Tied 6-6, Padres' Heath Bell facing 9-1-2
6-6	0	Cory Sullivan	Heath Bell	3-2 Walk
6-6	0	Kazuo Matsui	Heath Bell	0-2 Groundout: P-1B (Weak SS-2B); Sullivan to 2B
6-6	1	Troy Tulowitzki	Heath Bell	1-0 Groundout: P-1B (Weak SS)
6-6	2	Matt Holliday	Heath Bell	1-2 Strikeout Swinging

Top of the 9th, Padres Batting, Tied 6-6, Rockies' Manny Corpas facing 3-4-5
Manny Corpas replaces Brian Fuentes pitching and batting 7th
6-6	0	Kevin Kouzmanoff	Manny Corpas	0-0 Groundout: 2B-1B (SS-2B)
6-6	1	Adrian Gonzalez	Manny Corpas	1-1 Groundout: SS-1B (Weak 3B)
6-6	2	Khalil Greene	Manny Corpas	0-1 Flyball: RF (Deep CF-RF)

Bottom of the 9th, Rockies Batting, Tied 6-6, Padres' Heath Bell facing 4-5-6
6-6	0	Todd Helton	Heath Bell	1-2 Strikeout Swinging
6-6	1	Jamey Carroll	Heath Bell	1-1 Foul Popfly: 1B (1B into Foul Terr.)
6-6	2	Brad Hawpe	Heath Bell	3-1 Walk

Joe Koshansky pinch hits for Manny Corpas (P) batting 7th
6-6	2	Joe Koshansky	Heath Bell	0-2 Strikeout Swinging

Top of the 10th, Padres Batting, Tied 6-6, Rockies' Matt Herges facing 6-7-8
Matt Herges replaces Joe Koshansky (PH) pitching and batting 7th
Oscar Robles pinch hits for Heath Bell (P) batting 6th
6-6	0	Oscar Robles	Matt Herges	0-1 Groundout: 2B-1B (Weak 2B)
6-6	1	Geoff Blum	Matt Herges	1-0 Flyball: LF (Deep LF-CF)

Terrmel Sledge pinch hits for Brady Clark (CF) batting 8th
6-6	2	Terrmel Sledge	Matt Herges	3-0 Walk

Mike Cameron pinch runs for Terrmel Sledge (PH) batting 8th
6-6	2	Michael Barrett	Matt Herges	0-1 Single to LF (Line Drive to LF-CF); Cameron to 2B
6-6	2	Brian Giles	Matt Herges	2-2 Groundout: SS-2B/Forceout at 2B (Weak SS)

Bottom of the 10th, Rockies Batting, Tied 6-6, Padres' Doug Brocail facing 8-9-1
Doug Brocail replaces Oscar Robles (PH) pitching and batting 6th
Mike Cameron moves from PR to CF
6-6	0	Yorvit Torrealba	Doug Brocail	0-1 Groundout: 3B-1B (Weak 3B)
6-6	1	Cory Sullivan	Doug Brocail	2-2 Flyball: RF (Deep RF)
6-6	2	Kazuo Matsui	Doug Brocail	2-1 Popfly: SS (Deep 3B)

Top of the 11th, Padres Batting, Tied 6-6, Rockies' Matt Herges facing 2-3-4
6-6	0	Scott Hairston	Matt Herges	2-1 Reached on E5 (throw) (Ground Ball to Weak 3B)
6-6	0	Kevin Kouzmanoff	Matt Herges	0-0 Bunt Groundout: P-1B/Sacrifice; Hairston to 2B
6-6	1	Adrian Gonzalez	Matt Herges	3-0 Intentional Walk
6-6	1	Khalil Greene	Matt Herges	2-2 Ground Ball Double Play: 3B-1B (Weak 3B)

— Game 163 —

Bottom of the 11th, Rockies Batting, Tied 6-6, Padres' Doug Brocail facing 2-3-4
6-6 0 Troy Tulowitzki   Doug Brocail   0-0 Groundout: P-1B (Short 3B Line)
6-6 1 Matt Holliday   Doug Brocail   1-2 Strikeout Swinging
6-6 2 Todd Helton   Doug Brocail   3-1 Walk
6-6 2 Jamey Carroll   Doug Brocail   1-1 Single to RF (Line Drive); Helton to 2B
Joe Thatcher replaces Kevin Kouzmanoff (3B) pitching and batting 3rd
Morgan Ensberg replaces Doug Brocail (P) playing 3B batting 6th
6-6 2 Brad Hawpe   Joe Thatcher   2-2 Strikeout Swinging

Top of the 12th, Padres Batting, Tied 6-6, Rockies' Matt Herges facing 6-7-8
6-6 0 Morgan Ensberg   Matt Herges   3-2 Walk
6-6 0 Geoff Blum   Matt Herges   0-0 Bunt Groundout: 3B-1B/Sacrifice (Weak 3B); Ensberg to 2B
Brian Myrow pinch hits for Mike Cameron (CF) batting 8th
6-6 1 Brian Myrow   Matt Herges   2-2 Strikeout Swinging
6-6 2 Michael Barrett   Matt Herges   3-2 Groundout: SS-1B (Weak SS)

Bottom of the 12th, Rockies Batting, Tied 6-6, Padres' Joe Thatcher facing 7-8-9
Jason Lane replaces Brian Myrow (PH) playing CF batting 8th
Jeff Baker pinch hits for Matt Herges (P) batting 7th
6-6 0 Jeff Baker   Joe Thatcher   3-2 Strikeout Swinging
6-6 1 Yorvit Torrealba   Joe Thatcher   2-2 Flyball: CF (Deep CF)
6-6 2 Cory Sullivan   Joe Thatcher   1-2 Strikeout Swinging

Top of the 13th, Padres Batting, Tied 6-6, Rockies' Jorge Julio facing 1-2-3
Jorge Julio replaces Jeff Baker (PH) pitching and batting 7th
6-6 0 Brian Giles   Jorge Julio   3-1 Walk
6-6 0 Scott Hairston   Jorge Julio   1-0 Home Run (Fly Ball to Deep LF); Giles Scores
Chase Headley pinch hits for Joe Thatcher (P) batting 3rd
8-6 0 Chase Headley   Jorge Julio   1-1 Single to RF (Line Drive to Short CF-RF)
Ramon Ortiz replaces Jorge Julio pitching and batting 7th
8-6 0 Adrian Gonzalez   Ramon Ortiz   3-2 Strikeout Swinging
8-6 1 Khalil Greene   Ramon Ortiz   0-1 Flyball: LF (Deep LF)
8-6 2 Morgan Ensberg   Ramon Ortiz   1-0 Popfly: SS (Short CF)

Bottom of the 13th, Rockies Batting, Behind 6-8, Padres' Trevor Hoffman facing 1-2-3
Trevor Hoffman replaces Chase Headley (PH) pitching and batting 3rd
6-8 0 Kazuo Matsui   Trevor Hoffman 2-2 Double to CF (Line Drive to Deep CF-RF)
6-8 0 Troy Tulowitzki   Trevor Hoffman 3-2 Double to CF (Line Drive to Deep LF-CF); Matsui Scores
7-8 0 Matt Holliday   Trevor Hoffman 0-0 Triple to RF (Fly Ball to Deep RF); Tulowitzki Scores
8-8 0 Todd Helton   Trevor Hoffman 3-0 Intentional Walk
8-8 0 Jamey Carroll   Trevor Hoffman 0-0 Flyball: RF/Sacrifice Fly (Deep RF); Holliday Scores

SAN DIEGO PADRES	AB	R	H	RBI	BB	SO	BA
Brian Giles RF	5	2	1	1	2	0	.271
Scott Hairston LF	7	2	2	2	0	3	.243
Kevin Kouzmanoff 3B	5	0	1	0	0	1	.275
Joe Thatcher P	0	0	0	0	0	0	
Chase Headley PH	1	0	1	0	0	0	.222
Trevor Hoffman P	0	0	0	0	0	0	
Adrian Gonzalez 1B	6	1	3	4	1	2	.282
Khalil Greene SS	7	1	1	0	0	2	.254
Josh Bard C	4	0	2	0	0	0	.285
Heath Bell P	0	0	0	0	0	0	
Oscar Robles PH	1	0	0	0	0	0	.231
Doug Brocail P	0	0	0	0	0	0	.500
Morgan Ensberg 3B	1	0	0	0	1	0	.230
Geoff Blum 2B	4	1	1	0	1	1	.252
Brady Clark CF	4	0	1	1	0	0	.262
Terrmel Sledge PH	0	0	0	0	1	0	.210
Mike Cameron PR-CF	0	0	0	0	0	0	.242
Brian Myrow PH	1	0	0	0	0	1	.100
Jason Lane CF	0	0	0	0	0	0	.175
Jake Peavy P	3	1	1	0	0	0	.233
Michael Barrett C	3	0	1	0	0	1	.244
Team Totals	52	8	15	8	6	11	.288

2B: Josh Bard (27, off Josh Fogg); Adrian Gonzalez (46, off Josh Fogg); Brian Giles (27, off Brian Fuentes).
HR: Adrian Gonzalez (30, off Josh Fogg, 3rd inn, 3 on, 1 out to RF); Scott Hairston (11, off Jorge Julio, 13th inn, 1 on, 0 outs to LF).
SH: Kevin Kouzmanoff (2, off Matt Herges); Geoff Blum (3, off Matt Herges).
IBB: Geoff Blum (4, by Josh Fogg); Adrian Gonzalez (9, by Matt Herges).
TB: Adrian Gonzalez 7; Scott Hairston 5; Josh Bard 3; Brian Giles 2; Geoff Blum; Chase Headley; Kevin Kouzmanoff; Jake Peavy; Brady Clark; Khalil Greene; Michael Barrett.
GIDP: Khalil Greene (12).
RBI: Adrian Gonzalez 4 (100); Scott Hairston 2 (36); Brian Giles (51); Brady Clark (11).
2-out RBI: Brian Giles.
Team LOB: 13.
With RISP: 3 for 16.

GAME 163

COLORADO ROCKIES	AB	R	H	RBI	BB	SO	BA
Kazuo Matsui 2B	6	2	2	1	0	0	.288
Troy Tulowitzki SS	7	3	4	1	0	1	.291
Matt Holliday LF	6	1	2	2	1	3	.340
Todd Helton 1B	4	1	1	2	2	1	.320
Garrett Atkins 3B	3	0	2	1	1	1	.301
Jamey Carroll PR-3B	2	0	1	1	0	0	.225
Brad Hawpe RF	3	0	0	0	3	2	.291
Ryan Spilborghs CF	4	0	0	0	0	2	.299
Brian Fuentes P	0	0	0	0	0	0	
Manny Corpas P	0	0	0	0	0	0	
Joe Koshansky PH	1	0	0	0	0	1	.083
Matt Herges P	0	0	0	0	0	0	.000
Jeff Baker PH	1	0	0	0	0	1	.222
Jorge Julio P	0	0	0	0	0	0	
Ramon Ortiz P	0	0	0	0	0	0	.250
Yorvit Torrealba C	6	1	1	1	0	1	.255
Josh Fogg P	2	0	0	0	0	1	.132
Taylor Buchholz P	0	0	0	0	0	0	.130
Jeremy Affeldt P	0	0	0	0	0	0	
Ryan Speier P	0	0	0	0	0	0	
Seth Smith PH	1	1	1	0	0	0	.625
LaTroy Hawkins P	0	0	0	0	0	0	.000
Cory Sullivan CF	2	0	0	0	1	1	.286
Team Totals	48	9	14	9	8	15	.292

2B: Kazuo Matsui 2 (24, 1 off Trevor Hoffman, 1 off Jake Peavy); Troy Tulowitzki 2 (33, 1 off Trevor Hoffman, 1 off Jake Peavy); Garrett Atkins (35, off Jake Peavy).
3B: Seth Smith (1, off Jake Peavy); Troy Tulowitzki (5, off Jake Peavy); Matt Holliday (6, off Trevor Hoffman).
HR: Yorvit Torrealba (8, off Jake Peavy, 2nd inn, 0 on, 0 outs to LF); Todd Helton (17, off Jake Peavy, 3rd inn, 0 on, 1 out to RF).
SF: Todd Helton (7, off Jake Peavy); Kazuo Matsui (1, off Jake Peavy); Jamey Carroll (3, off Trevor Hoffman).
IBB: Brad Hawpe 2 (11, 2 by Jake Peavy); Todd Helton (16, by Trevor Hoffman).
TB: Troy Tulowitzki 8; Yorvit Torrealba 4; Todd Helton 4; Kazuo Matsui 4; Matt Holliday 4; Garrett Atkins 3; Seth Smith 3; Jamey Carroll.
RBI: Todd Helton 2 (91); Matt Holliday 2 (137); Garrett Atkins (111); Troy Tulowitzki (99); Kazuo Matsui (37); Yorvit Torrealba (47); Jamey Carroll (22).
Team LOB: 13.
With RISP: 5 for 15.

DP: 1. Jamey Carroll-Todd Helton. E: Jamey Carroll (4).

SAN DIEGO PADRES	IP	H	R	ER	BB	SO	HR	ERA	BF	Pit	Str
Jake Peavy	6.1	10	6	6	4	6	2	2.54	33	118	68
Heath Bell	2.2	0	0	0	2	5	0	2.02	10	42	26
Doug Brocail	1.2	1	0	0	1	1	0	3.05	7	24	14
Joe Thatcher	1.1	0	0	0	0	3	0	1.29	4	20	12
Trevor Hoffman, BS (7), L (4-5)	0.1	3	3	3	1	0	0	2.98	5	19	10
Team Totals	12.1	14	9	9	8	15	2	6.57	59	223	130

COLORADO ROCKIES	IP	H	R	ER	BB	SO	HR	ERA	BF	Pit	Str
Josh Fogg	4	8	5	5	2	5	1	4.94	22	75	49
Taylor Buchholz	1.1	1	0	0	0	1	0	4.23	5	13	12
Jeremy Affeldt	0.1	0	0	0	0	0	0	3.51	1	7	4
Ryan Speier	0.1	0	0	0	0	1	0	4.00	1	6	3
LaTroy Hawkins, H (17)	1	1	0	0	0	1	0	3.42	4	15	9
Brian Fuentes, BS (7)	1	2	1	1	0	1	0	3.08	5	14	12
Manny Corpas	1	0	0	0	0	0	0	2.08	3	6	5
Matt Herges	3	1	0	0	3	1	0	2.96	13	47	23
Jorge Julio	0	2	2	2	1	0	1	5.23	3	10	4
Ramon Ortiz, W (5-4)	1	0	0	0	0	1	0	5.45	3	10	6
Team Totals	13	15	8	8	6	11	2	5.54	60	203	127

Josh Fogg faced 1 batter in the 5th inning.
Jorge Julio faced 3 batters in the 13th inning.
Balks: None.
WP: Jeremy Affeldt (6); Brian Fuentes (2).
HBP: None.
IBB: Josh Fogg (7; Geoff Blum); Trevor Hoffman (5; Todd Helton); Matt Herges (2; Adrian Gonzalez);
 Jake Peavy 2 (5; Brad Hawpe, Brad Hawpe).
Pickoffs: None.

Umpires: HP - Tim McClelland, 1B - Ed Montague, 2B - Tim Tschida, 3B - Chuck Meriwether, LF -
 Fieldin Culbreth, RF - Jim Wolf.
Time of Game: 4:40.
Attendance: 48,404.
Field Condition: Unknown.
Start Time Weather: 75° F, Wind 3mph out to Centerfield, Cloudy.

Courtesy Baseball-Reference.com

— GAME 163 —

Appendix
2007 Rockies Game-by-Game

Gm	Date	Opp	W/L	Runs For	Runs Against	Inn	W-L	Rank	GB
1	Monday, Apr 2	ARI	L	6	8		0-1	4	1.0
2	Tuesday, Apr 3	ARI	W	4	3	11	1-1	2	0.5
3	Wednesday, Apr 4	ARI	W	11	4		2-1	2	0.5
4	Friday, Apr 6	@ SDP	W	4	3		3-1	1	up 0.5
5	Saturday, Apr 7	@ SDP	L	2	3		3-2	2	0.5
6	Sunday, Apr 8	@ SDP	L	1	2	10	3-3	4	1.5
7	Monday, Apr 9	@ LAD	W	6	3		4-3	3	1.5
8	Tuesday, Apr 10	@ LAD	L	1	2		4-4	4	2.5
9	Wednesday, Apr 11	@ LAD	L	0	3		4-5	4	2.5
10	Friday, Apr 13	@ ARI	W	6	3		5-5	4	2.0
11	Saturday, Apr 14	@ ARI	L	4	5		5-6	4	2.5
12	Sunday, Apr 15	@ ARI	L	4	6		5-7	4	3.5
13	Monday, Apr 16	SFG	L	0	8		5-8	4	4.0
14	Tuesday, Apr 17	SFG	W	5	3		6-8	4	4.0
15	Wednesday, Apr 18	LAD	W	7	2		7-8	4	3.0
16	Thursday, Apr 19	LAD	L	1	8		7-9	4	4.0
17	Friday, Apr 20	SDP	L	1	11		7-10	5	5.0
18	Saturday, Apr 21	SDP	L	3	7		7-11	5	6.0
19	Sunday, Apr 22	SDP	W	4	2		8-11	5	5.0
20	Monday, Apr 23	@ NYM	L	1	6		8-12	5	5.5
21	Tuesday, Apr 24	@ NYM	L	1	2	12	8-13	5	5.5
22	Wednesday, Apr 25	@ NYM	W	11	5		9-13	5	4.5
23	Friday, Apr 27	ATL	L	7	9		9-14	5	5.0
24	Saturday, Apr 28	ATL	L	2	6		9-15	5	5.0
25	Sunday, Apr 29	ATL	W	9	7	11	10-15	5	5.0
26	Monday, Apr 30	@ SFG	L	5	9		10-16	5	5.5
27	Tuesday, May 1	@ SFG	W	9	7		11-16	5	5.0
28	Wednesday, May 2	@ SFG	L	3	5		11-17	5	6.0
29	Friday, May 4	@ CIN	W	6	5	11	12-17	5	5.0
30	Saturday, May 5	@ CIN	W	9	7		13-17	5	5.0
31	Sunday, May 6	@ CIN	L	3	9		13-18	5	5.0
32	Monday, May 7	@ STL	W	3	2		14-18	5	5.0

33	Tuesday, May 8	@ STL	L	1	4		14-19	5	5.0
34	Wednesday, May 9	@ STL	L	2	9		14-20	5	6.0
35	Thursday, May 10	SFG	W	5	3		15-20	5	5.0
36	Friday, May 11	SFG	L	3	8		15-21	5	6.0
37	Saturday, May 12	SFG	W	6	2		16-21	5	6.0
38	Sunday, May 13	SFG	L	2	15		16-22	5	7.0
39	Tuesday, May 15	ARI	L	0	3		16-23	5	7.5
40	Wednesday, May 16	ARI	W	5	3		17-23	5	7.5
41	Thursday, May 17	ARI	L	1	3		17-24	5	8.0
42	Friday, May 18	KCR	L	2	5		17-25	5	8.0
43	Saturday, May 19	KCR	W	6	4		18-25	5	7.0
44	Sunday, May 20	KCR	L	5	10	12	18-26	5	7.0
45	Monday, May 21	@ ARI	L	5	6		18-27	5	7.0
46	Tuesday, May 22	@ ARI	W	3	1		19-27	5	7.0
47	Wednesday, May 23	@ ARI	W	2	0		20-27	5	7.0
48	Friday, May 25	@ SFG	W	5	3		21-27	5	7.0
49	Saturday, May 26	@ SFG	W	6	1		22-27	5	6.0
50	Sunday, May 27	@ SFG	W	6	4	10	23-27	5	6.0
51	Monday, May 28	STL	W	6	2		24-27	5	5.5
52	Tuesday, May 29	STL	W	8	3		25-27	4	5.5
53	Wednesday, May 30	STL	L	4	8		25-28	5	6.5
54	Thursday, May 31	STL	L	3	7		25-29	5	6.5
55	Friday, Jun 1	CIN	L	2	4		25-30	5	7.5
56	Saturday, Jun 2	CIN	W	4	1		26-30	5	6.5
57	Sunday, Jun 3	CIN	W	10	9	10	27-30	4	6.5
58	Tuesday, Jun 5	HOU	L	1	4		27-31	5	7.5
59	Wednesday, Jun 6	HOU	W	8	7		28-31	4	7.5
60	Thursday, Jun 7	HOU	W	7	6		29-31	4	7.5
61	Friday, Jun 8	@ BAL	L	2	4		29-32	4	7.5
62	Saturday, Jun 9	@ BAL	W	3	2	10	30-32	4	6.5
63	Sunday, Jun 10	@ BAL	W	6	1		31-32	4	5.5
64	Tuesday, Jun 12	@ BOS	L	1	2		31-33	4	5.5
65	Wednesday, Jun 13	@ BOS	W	12	2		32-33	4	5.5
66	Thursday, Jun 14	@ BOS	W	7	1		33-33	4	5.5
67	Friday, Jun 15	TBD	W	12	2		34-33	4	5.0
68	Saturday, Jun 16	TBD	W	10	5		35-33	4	4.5
69	Sunday, Jun 17	TBD	L	4	7		35-34	4	5.5
70	Tuesday, Jun 19	NYY	W	3	1		36-34	4	5.5
71	Wednesday, Jun 20	NYY	W	6	1		37-34	4	4.5
72	Thursday, Jun 21	NYY	W	4	3		38-34	4	3.5
73	Friday, Jun 22	@ TOR	L	8	9	10	38-35	4	4.0
74	Saturday, Jun 23	@ TOR	L	6	11		38-36	4	4.5
75	Sunday, Jun 24	@ TOR	L	0	5		38-37	4	5.5
76	Monday, Jun 25	@ CHC	L	9	10		38-38	4	5.5
77	Tuesday, Jun 26	@ CHC	L	5	8		38-39	4	6.0

— Game 163 —

#	Date	Opp	W/L	R	RA	Inn	Rec	Pos	GB
78	Wednesday, Jun 27	@ CHC	L	4	6		38-40	4	6.5
79	Thursday, Jun 28	@ HOU	L	5	8	11	38-41	4	7.0
80	Friday, Jun 29	@ HOU	L	8	9		38-42	4	8.0
81	Saturday, Jun 30	@ HOU	W	5	0		39-42	4	8.0
82	Sunday, Jul 1	@ HOU	L	0	12		39-43	4	8.0
83	Monday, Jul 2	NYM	W	6	2		40-43	4	8.0
84	Tuesday, Jul 3	NYM	W	11	3		41-43	4	7.0
85	Wednesday, Jul 4	NYM	W	17	7		42-43	4	7.0
86	Friday, Jul 6	PHI	W	7	6	11	43-43	4	5.5
87	Saturday, Jul 7	PHI	W	6	3		44-43	4	5.5
88	Sunday, Jul 8	PHI	L	4	8		44-44	4	5.5
89	Friday, Jul 13	@ MIL	W	10	6		45-44	4	4.5
90	Saturday, Jul 14	@ MIL	L	1	2	10	45-45	4	5.5
91	Sunday, Jul 15	@ MIL	L	3	4		45-46	4	6.5
92	Monday, Jul 16	@ PIT	W	10	8		46-46	4	6.5
93	Tuesday, Jul 17	@ PIT	W	6	2		47-46	4	5.5
94	Wednesday, Jul 18	@ PIT	W	5	3		48-46	4	5.5
95	Thursday, Jul 19	@ WSN	L	4	5	10	48-47	4	5.5
96	Friday, Jul 20	@ WSN	W	3	1		49-47	3	4.5
97	Saturday, Jul 21	@ WSN	L	0	3		49-48	4	5.5
98	Sunday, Jul 22	@ WSN	L	0	3		49-49	4	5.5
99	Monday, Jul 23	SDP	W	7	5		50-49	4	5.5
100	Tuesday, Jul 24	SDP	L	3	5		50-50	4	5.5
101	Wednesday, Jul 25	SDP	W	10	2		51-50	4	4.5
102	Thursday, Jul 26	LAD	L	4	5		51-51	4	5.5
103	Saturday, Jul 28	LAD	W	6	2		52-51	4	4.5
104	Sunday, Jul 29	LAD	W	9	6		53-51	4	3.5
105	Tuesday, Jul 31	@ FLA	W	6	3		54-51	4	3.5
106	Wednesday, Aug 1	@ FLA	L	3	4		54-52	4	4.5
107	Thursday, Aug 2	@ FLA	W	4	3		55-52	4	3.5
108	Friday, Aug 3	@ ATL	W	9	2		56-52	4	3.5
109	Saturday, Aug 4	@ ATL	L	4	6		56-53	4	4.5
110	Sunday, Aug 5	@ ATL	L	5	6	10	56-54	4	5.5
111	Monday, Aug 6	MIL	W	6	2		57-54	4	5.0
112	Tuesday, Aug 7	MIL	W	11	4		58-54	3	4.0
113	Wednesday, Aug 8	MIL	W	19	4		59-54	3	4.0
114	Thursday, Aug 9	CHC	L	2	10		59-55	3	5.0
115	Friday, Aug 10	CHC	L	2	6		59-56	4	6.0
116	Saturday, Aug 11	CHC	W	15	2		60-56	3	6.0
117	Sunday, Aug 12	CHC	W	6	3		61-56	3	5.0
118	Tuesday, Aug 14	@ SDP	L	0	8		61-57	3	5.0
119	Wednesday, Aug 15	@ SDP	W	3	0		62-57	3	5.0
120	Thursday, Aug 16	@ SDP	L	9	11		62-58	3	6.0
121	Friday, Aug 17	@ LAD	L	4	6		62-59	4	7.0
122	Saturday, Aug 18	@ LAD	W	7	4	14	63-59	3	7.0

#	Date	Opp	W/L	R	RA	Inn	Rec	Pos	GB
123	Sunday, Aug 19	@ LAD	L	3	4		63-60	4	7.0
124	Monday, Aug 20	PIT	L	2	4	11	63-61	4	7.0
125	Tuesday, Aug 21	PIT	W	9	2		64-61	3	6.0
126	Wednesday, Aug 22	PIT	L	2	11		64-62	4	7.0
127	Thursday, Aug 23	PIT	L	1	5		64-63	4	7.5
128	Friday, Aug 24	WSN	W	6	5		65-63	4	6.5
129	Saturday, Aug 25	WSN	W	5	1		66-63	3	6.5
130	Sunday, Aug 26	WSN	W	10	5		67-63	3	6.5
131	Monday, Aug 27	@ SFG	L	1	4		67-64	4	6.5
132	Tuesday, Aug 28	@ SFG	L	1	3		67-65	4	6.5
133	Wednesday, Aug 29	@ SFG	W	8	0		68-65	4	5.5
134	Friday, Aug 31	@ ARI	W	7	3	10	69-65	4	5.0
135	Saturday, Sep 1	@ ARI	L	7	13		69-66	4	6.0
136	Sunday, Sep 2	@ ARI	W	4	3		70-66	4	5.0
137	Monday, Sep 3	SFG	W	7	4		71-66	4	5.0
138	Tuesday, Sep 4	SFG	W	6	5		72-66	4	4.0
139	Wednesday, Sep 5	SFG	L	3	5		72-67	4	5.0
140	Friday, Sep 7	SDP	W	10	4		73-67	4	5.0
141	Saturday, Sep 8	SDP	L	1	3		73-68	4	6.0
142	Sunday, Sep 9	SDP	W	4	2		74-68	4	6.0
143	Monday, Sep 10	@ PHI	L	5	6	10	74-69	4	7.0
144	Tuesday, Sep 11	@ PHI	W	8	2		75-69	3	6.0
145	Wednesday, Sep 12	@ PHI	W	12	0		76-69	3	6.0
146	Thursday, Sep 13	@ PHI	L	4	12		76-70	4	6.5
147	Friday, Sep 14	FLA	L	6	7		76-71	4	6.5
148	Saturday, Sep 15	FLA	L	2	10		76-72	4	6.5
149	Sunday, Sep 16	FLA	W	13	0		77-72	4	6.5
150	Tuesday, Sep 18 (1)	LAD	W	3	1		78-72	3	5.5
151	Tuesday, Sep 18 (2)	LAD	W	9	8		79-72	3	5.5
152	Wednesday, Sep 19	LAD	W	6	5		80-72	3	5.5
153	Thursday, Sep 20	LAD	W	9	4		81-72	3	5.0
154	Friday, Sep 21	@ SDP	W	2	1	14	82-72	3	5.0
155	Saturday, Sep 22	@ SDP	W	6	2		83-72	3	5.0
156	Sunday, Sep 23	@ SDP	W	7	3		84-72	3	4.0
157	Tuesday, Sep 25	@ LAD	W	9	7		85-72	3	3.0
158	Wednesday, Sep 26	@ LAD	W	2	0		86-72	3	2.0
159	Thursday, Sep 27	@ LAD	W	10	4		87-72	3	2.0
160	Friday, Sep 28	ARI	L	2	4		87-73	3	3.0
161	Saturday, Sep 29	ARI	W	11	1		88-73	3	2.0
162	Sunday, Sep 30	ARI	W	4	3		89-73	2	1.0
163	Monday, Oct 1	SDP	W	9	8	13	90-73	2	0.5

Courtesy Baseball-Reference.com

— GAME 163 —

Appendix
2007 Rockies Team Stats

Pos	Name	Age	G	PA	AB	R	H	2B	3B	HR	RBI	SB	CS	BB	SO	BA	OBP	SLG
C	Yorvit Torrealba	28	113	443	396	47	101	22	1	8	47	2	1	34	73	.255	.323	.376
1B	Todd Helton*	33	154	682	557	86	178	42	2	17	91	0	1	116	74	.320	.434	.494
2B	Kazuo Matsui#	31	104	453	410	84	118	24	6	4	37	32	4	34	69	.288	.342	.405
SS	Troy Tulowitzki	22	155	682	609	104	177	33	5	24	99	7	6	57	130	.291	.359	.479
3B	Garrett Atkins	27	157	684	605	83	182	35	1	25	111	3	1	67	96	.301	.367	.486
LF	Matt Holliday	27	158	713	636	120	216	50	6	36	137	11	4	63	126	.340	.405	.607
CF	Willy Taveras	25	97	408	372	64	119	13	2	2	24	33	9	21	55	.320	.367	.382
RF	Brad Hawpe*	28	152	606	516	80	150	33	4	29	116	0	2	81	137	.291	.387	.539
CF	Ryan Spilborghs	27	97	300	264	40	79	14	1	11	51	4	1	28	45	.299	.363	.485
2B	Jamey Carroll	33	108	268	227	45	51	9	1	2	22	6	2	28	34	.225	.317	.300
C	Chris Iannetta	24	67	234	197	22	43	8	3	4	27	0	0	29	58	.218	.330	.350
UT	Jeff Baker	26	85	159	144	17	32	2	2	4	12	0	0	13	40	.222	.296	.347
CF	Cory Sullivan*	27	72	153	140	19	40	6	1	2	14	2	0	9	25	.286	.336	.386
CF	Steve Finley*	42	43	102	94	9	17	3	0	1	2	0	0	8	4	.181	.245	.245
2B	Omar Quintanilla*	25	27	75	70	6	16	4	0	0	5	0	0	5	15	.229	.280	.286
3B	Ian Stewart*	22	35	46	43	3	9	4	0	1	9	0	0	1	17	.209	.261	.372
UT	John Mabry*	36	28	39	34	4	4	1	0	1	5	0	0	5	10	.118	.231	.235
UT	Clint Barmes	28	27	39	37	5	8	3	0	0	0	0	0	1	13	.216	.237	.297
C	Geronimo Gil	31	5	16	14	1	1	0	0	0	0	0	0	1	5	.071	.133	.071
1B	Joe Koshansky*	25	17	15	12	0	1	1	0	0	2	0	0	2	5	.083	.200	.167
RF	Seth Smith*	24	7	8	8	4	5	0	1	0	0	0	0	0	1	.625	.625	.875
OF	Sean Barker	27	3	3	2	0	0	0	0	0	0	0	0	0	1	.000	.333	.000
C	Edwin Bellorin	25	3	2	2	0	0	0	0	0	0	0	0	0	0	.000	.000	.000
P	Jeff Francis*	26	33	79	64	2	12	3	0	0	3	0	0	2	20	.188	.212	.234
P	Josh Fogg	30	28	63	53	3	7	0	0	0	1	0	0	1	19	.132	.148	.132
P	Aaron Cook	28	23	60	42	8	10	3	0	0	1	0	0	4	14	.238	.319	.310
P	Jason Hirsh	25	17	34	31	0	3	0	0	0	2	0	0	1	17	.097	.125	.097
P	Ubaldo Jimenez	23	15	31	24	0	2	0	0	0	0	0	0	3	6	.083	.185	.083
P	Taylor Buchholz	25	38	26	23	0	3	0	0	0	1	0	0	2	11	.130	.200	.130
P	Rodrigo Lopez	31	13	24	22	0	1	0	0	0	0	0	0	1	13	.045	.087	.045
P	Franklin Morales*	21	8	15	13	1	4	0	0	0	1	0	0	1	5	.308	.357	.308

Pos	Name																	
P	Elmer Dessens	36	5	9	6	2	0	0	0	0	0	0	0	2	2	.000	.250	.000
P	Mark Redman*	33	5	8	8	0	0	0	0	0	0	0	0	0	1	.000	.000	.000
P	Matt Herges*	37	35	6	6	0	0	0	0	0	0	0	0	0	5	.000	.000	.000
P	Ramon Ortiz	34	10	2	1	1	1	0	0	0	1	0	0	1	0	1.000	1.000	1.000
P	Byung-Hyun Kim	28	3	2	2	0	0	0	0	0	0	0	0	0	1	.000	.000	.000
P	Tom Martin*	37	23	2	1	0	0	0	0	0	0	0	0	0	0	.000	.000	.000
P	Alberto Arias	23	6	2	2	0	0	0	0	0	0	0	0	0	2	.000	.000	.000
P	Tim Harikkala	35	1	1	1	0	1	0	0	1	0	0	0	0	0	1.000	1.000	1.000
P	Zach McClellan	28	12	1	1	0	0	0	0	0	0	0	0	0	1	.000	.000	.000
P	LaTroy Hawkins	34	59	1	1	0	0	0	0	0	0	0	0	0	1	.000	.000	.000
P	Denny Bautista	26	9	1	1	0	0	0	0	0	0	0	0	0	1	.000	.000	.000
P	Jorge Julio	28	54	1	0	0	0	0	0	0	0	0	0	1	0		1.000	
P	Ramon Ramirez	25	22	0	0	0	0	0	0	0	0	0	0	0	0			
P	Juan Morillo	23	4	0	0	0	0	0	0	0	0	0	0	0	0			
P	Manny Corpas	24	74	0	0	0	0	0	0	0	0	0	0	0	0			
P	Jeremy Affeldt*	28	72	0	0	0	0	0	0	0	0	0	0	0	0			
P	Brian Fuentes*	31	61	0	0	0	0	0	0	0	0	0	0	0	0			
P	Ryan Speier	27	20	0	0	0	0	0	0	0	0	0	0	0	0			
P	Bobby Keppel	25	4	0	0	0	0	0	0	0	0	0	0	0	0			
P	Darren Clarke	26	2	0	0	0	0	0	0	0	0	0	0	0	0			
P	Dan Serafini#	33	3	0	0	0	0	0	0	0	0	0	0	0	0			
P	Josh Newman*	25	2	0	0	0	0	0	0	0	0	0	0	0	0			
	Team Totals	27.9	163	6498	5691	860	1591	313	36	171	823	100	31	622	1152	.280	.354	.437

* - bats left-handed, # - bats both

— GAME 163 —

Name	Age	W	L	W-L%	ERA	G	GS	CG	ShO	SV	IP	H	R	ER	HR	BB	SO	WHIP
Jeff Francis*	26	17	9	.654	4.22	34	34	1	1	0	215.1	234	103	101	25	63	165	1.379
Aaron Cook	28	8	7	.533	4.12	25	25	2	0	0	166.0	178	87	76	15	44	61	1.337
Josh Fogg	30	10	9	.526	4.94	30	29	0	0	0	165.2	194	99	91	23	59	94	1.527
Jason Hirsh	25	5	7	.417	4.81	19	19	1	0	0	112.1	103	63	60	18	48	75	1.344
Ubaldo Jimenez	23	4	4	.500	4.28	15	15	0	0	0	82.0	70	46	39	10	37	68	1.305
Rodrigo Lopez	31	5	4	.556	4.42	14	14	0	0	0	79.1	83	43	39	11	21	43	1.311
Brian Fuentes*	31	3	5	.375	3.08	64	0	0	0	20	61.1	46	26	21	6	23	56	1.125
Manny Corpas	24	4	2	.667	2.08	78	0	0	0	19	78.0	63	20	18	6	20	58	1.064
Jeremy Affeldt*	28	4	3	.571	3.51	75	0	0	0	0	59.0	47	26	23	3	33	46	1.356
LaTroy Hawkins	34	2	5	.286	3.42	62	0	0	0	0	55.1	52	21	21	6	16	29	1.229
Jorge Julio	28	0	3	.000	3.93	58	0	0	0	0	52.2	50	25	23	6	20	50	1.329
Taylor Buchholz	25	6	5	.545	4.23	41	8	0	0	0	93.2	105	47	44	8	20	61	1.335
Matt Herges	37	5	1	.833	2.96	35	0	0	0	0	48.2	34	17	16	4	15	30	1.007
Franklin Morales*	21	3	2	.600	3.43	8	8	0	0	0	39.1	34	15	15	2	14	26	1.220
Tom Martin*	37	0	0		4.91	26	0	0	0	0	25.2	32	14	14	4	9	10	1.597
Mark Redman*	33	2	0	1.000	3.20	5	3	0	0	0	19.2	21	8	7	2	6	14	1.373
Elmer Dessens	36	1	1	.500	7.58	5	5	0	0	0	19.0	21	16	16	3	9	10	1.579
Ryan Speier	27	3	1	.750	4.00	20	0	0	0	0	18.0	20	8	8	1	8	13	1.556
Ramon Ramirez	25	2	2	.500	8.31	22	0	0	0	0	17.1	21	16	16	2	6	15	1.558
Zach McClellan	28	1	0	1.000	5.79	12	0	0	0	0	14.0	20	9	9	0	5	13	1.786
Ramon Ortiz	34	1	0	1.000	7.62	10	0	0	0	0	13.0	15	11	11	4	7	7	1.692
Denny Bautista	26	2	1	.667	12.46	9	1	0	0	0	8.2	18	12	12	0	4	8	2.538
Alberto Arias	23	1	0	1.000	4.91	6	0	0	0	0	7.1	8	4	4	1	5	3	1.773
Byung-Hyun Kim	28	1	2	.333	10.50	3	1	0	0	0	6.0	6	7	7	2	4	2	1.667
Bobby Keppel	25	0	0		11.25	4	0	0	0	0	4.0	6	5	5	1	3	1	2.250
Juan Morillo	23	0	0		9.82	4	0	0	0	0	3.2	3	4	4	1	1	3	1.091
Tim Harikkala	35	0	0		8.10	1	1	0	0	0	3.1	9	3	3	0	1	2	3.000
Josh Newman*	25	0	0		4.50	2	0	0	0	0	2.0	2	1	1	0	0	3	1.000
Darren Clarke	26	0	0		0.00	2	0	0	0	0	1.1	2	0	0	0	1	1	2.250
Dan Serafini*	33	0	0		54.00	3	0	0	0	0	0.1	0	2	2	0	2	0	6.000
Team Totals	27.9	90	73	.552	4.32	163	163	4	1	39	1472.0	1497	758	706	164	504	967	1.359

Courtesy Baseball-Reference.com

 DENNY DRESSMAN is a former award-winning reporter, editor and senior executive who concluded a 42-year newspaper career in 2007. A member of the Denver Press Club Hall of Fame and a past president of both the Colorado Press Association and the Colorado Authors' League, he is the author of 12 other books. His biography of the late Grambling football coach, Eddie Robinson, in the context of Jim Crow segregation and the Civil Rights Movement of the early 1960s, was a Colorado Book Award finalist. He lives in Denver with his wife Melanie.